25 Chapters of My Life

*Grand Duchess Olga Alexandrovna
of Russia*

25 Chapters of My Life

*Grand Duchess Olga Alexandrovna
of Russia*

PAUL KULIKOVSKY
KAREN ROTH-NICHOLLS
SUE WOOLMANS

Librario

Published by

Librario Publishing Ltd.

ISBN: 978-1-906775-16-2

Copies can be ordered via the Internet
www.librario.com

or from:

Brough House, Milton Brodie, Kinloss
Moray IV36 2UA
Tel/Fax No 00 44 (0)1343 850 617

Printed and bound in the UK

Typeset by 3btype.com

Contents

Preface

by Xenia Kulikovsky Nielsen

I had an extraordinary grandmother, she was altogether incredibly lovely, I never gave a thought to her being an Imperial Grand Duchess, just that she was a warm and generous person. She was always kindness itself to anyone in need.

I lived a lot with my paternal grandmother from the time I was born till she died. Actually, I spent more time with my grandparents than I did with my parents. *Knudsminde*, my grandmother's home in Ballerup, Denmark, was a big and cosy house with soft couches and huge upholstered arm chairs. They were perfect for a child to play hide-and-seek behind or to cuddle up in for a nap. I always had the feeling that we were surrounded by people – our guests or the farm workers. There was a lot of life in that house.

Even though my grandmother had lived through many tragedies and two wars, she was a positive person, who preferred not to look back upon the past. She took great interest in life and the people around her, and the town of Ballerup meant a lot to her. I often accompanied her when there was shopping to be done in Ballerup. I especially loved the dairy shop and their butter-tubs; they had such a fine stamp for the butter. My grandmother did not give much thought to her clothes and when we went into town she would often wear Wellingtons as they were especially easy to put on.

Grandmother's great passion was to paint. Not a single day would pass without her having a brush in her hand. She preferred doing watercolours but oil paintings also came into being. Her pictures were mainly of the neighbourhood or her own garden.

However, our lives underwent a change after the war and the German occupation and the feeling of security, which the family had found in Denmark, was gone. The once so distant Soviet Union had now come very close, when they occupied the Danish island Bornholm, and in 1948 my family no longer felt that they dared stayed on in Denmark. I was only seven years old and was, of course, not consulted, but I understood that they feared that my grandmother would be kidnapped by the Soviet Union. The Danish government did not want to or was not able to guarantee her safety, which is why the whole family more or less had to flee to Canada.

Canada reminded my grandparents very much of Russia and we felt at ease there, but it was a long way from Denmark and we missed the rest of the family and our friends there.

My grandfather, Nicholas Kulikovsky, died in 1958. My grandmother never got over his death; he was the love of her life. She died on 24th November 1960 – the last Grand Duchess of Russia.

Xenia Kulikovsky Nielsen

Introduction

by Paul Kulikovsky

When my great-grandparents, the Grand Duchess Olga Alexandrovna of Russia and Colonel Nicholas Kulikovsky, celebrated their Silver Wedding anniversary on November 17th, 1941, they were surrounded by a great deal of publicity. They had a story to tell and agreed to be interviewed in their home Knudsminde in Ballerup, Denmark. Two journalists came to Knudsminde on December 5th, Kaj Holbech from the magazine Billed-Bladet and Ralph Buch from the publication B.T. (Berlingske Tidende). A detailed article with pictures from the Grand Duchess's life and Silver Wedding anniversary was subsequently published in Billed-Bladet. The interview was supplemented by the Grand Duchess's handwritten recollections, which she jotted down during the following weeks. She wrote in the language which came to mind, either in Danish or English often jumping from one language to the other in the self-same sentence and adding French expressions. These reminiscences appeared in Danish in the publication BT between March 22nd and April 21st, 1942 under the title *Storfyrstindens Erindringer – the Grand Duchess's Memoirs*.

In 2005 my mother, Xenia Kulikovsky Nielsen – the Grand Duchess's granddaughter – gave permission for these memoirs to be published in book-form in Copenhagen, Denmark, under the title *Storfyrstinde Olga – 25 kapitler af mit liv* (*Grand Duchess Olga – 25 Chapters of my Life*). The first edition was published in September 2006 and the second in April 2007. This book was sold widely in Scandinavia and led me to believe that it would also be of interest to readers in the English-speaking world.

In order to focus on my great-grandmother as a person it was decided to let her tell her own story. This English edition is therefore not merely a translation of the Danish book but is primarily based on the Grand Duchess's handwritten notes. Some of these notes were omitted in the Danish book; they now appear in full in this edition. Whenever the Grand Duchess wrote in English, her notes – which appear in italics in this book – have been literally transcribed with some corrections of spelling errors and minor adjustments made for the sake of clarity. The Danish notes have been translated by Karen Roth-Nicholls. The part of the text, which is not covered by the notes, is based on the Danish book.

While working on this book, a number of details came to light, among others a series of letters which the Grand Duchess wrote to her nieces, the daughters of Emperor Nicholas II, in Russian during the time she spent as a nurse in the First World War. Those of the letters, which are relevant to the twenty-five chapters are placed at the end of the respective chapters and have also been translated by Karen Roth-Nicholls.

There have been 2 books previously published in English about the life of Grand Duchess Olga Alexandrovna. The first one in 1964 by Ian Vorres, *The Last Grand Duchess* and the second in 1999 by Patricia Phenix, *Olga Romanov – Russia's Last Grand Duchess*. The first book was mainly based on interviews with my great-grandmother and the second mainly on archival research. What makes this third book special is that this time it is the Grand Duchess's own words, her phrases, her choice of what to include and what to omit, and her way of telling her own story!

Enjoy the reading!

Paul Kulikovsky

DATING

Russia used the Old Style Julian calendar until February 1st 1918. This was twelve days behind the west in the nineteenth century and thirteen days behind in the twentieth century. Where known, it has been chosen to indicate both the Old Julian Style and the New Gregorian Style.

Grand Duchess Olga Alexandrovna of Russia and Colonel Nicholas Kulikovsky
in their living room at Knudsminde on their Silver Wedding anniversary,
November 17th, 1941.

CHAPTER I

With Europe's Grandfather

The love of my youth, my dear husband, Colonel Nicholas Kulikovsky, and I were able to celebrate our Silver Wedding anniversary on November 17th last year [1941]. Twenty-two of those twenty-five years were spent in Denmark, and for half of those years we have lived on our farm 'Knudsminde' near Ballerup. At a wedding celebration, one only looks into the future, but at a Silver Wedding, one also looks back. We do not know how many days and years we have left, but we know the time that lies behind us. Let me try to pull the curtain a little aside to reveal a life which has not only brought both grief, ups and downs and disappointments, but also much happiness.

If we had not already been aware of the many friends we have, we found out on the day of our Silver Wedding. We are infinitely grateful for all the kindnesses with which we were met. And it didn't stop on the great day itself. In the days following our Silver Wedding, congratulations kept on arriving from known and unknown friends. Among the many greetings there was also one from a man in South Jutland, whom we had never met. He wrote that he had fought in the last World War and that he had been taken prisoner on the Russian front in April 1916 – the same year we were married. He went on to say that he had been confined in a Russian prison camp. He had brought a cavalry sabre home from Russia, and now he just wanted to ask if it would please the Colonel to receive this sabre as a present from an unknown friend. I am telling this little story because I want to stress already, now, in this very first chapter that life has taught me that love is stronger than hate. I know that evil is a powerful force, but I firmly believe that goodness will triumph even though at times it is long in coming and puts human patience and faith to hard tests.

My father was proclaimed Emperor the year before I was born. I was the youngest of us brothers and sisters. My late brother Nicholas was 14 when I was born, George was 12, my sister Xenia 7 and Michael 3½. I grew up with 'Misha' without playmates of my own age, but we did not miss them, since the sailors and soldiers, who served at the Palace, were always ready to play with us. Many of them had fought in the war against Turkey, and they would talk away about their experiences, which were exciting and colourful – perhaps even a little too exciting and colourful for a young and impressionable child's soul. My childhood home was in Gatchina, which lies 45 km from St. Petersburg. It is a big palace with over 600 rooms. The summer was normally spent in Peterhof, which lies on the shores of the Gulf of Finland. It is a small residential suburb, which more or less means the same to St. Petersburg as Windsor does to Buckingham Palace. We children were very fond of being there, but Gatchina was the 'home of my heart'.

One summer's day I had an experience which made quite a strong impression on my childish mind. There was a Danish naval visit in Peterhof and a group of young cadets paid my parents a visit. Out in the park there was a high mast, which was encircled by a very strong net of the same type as is used in a circus when the acrobats perform. It was fun for us children to climb up the mast and jump down from the height which suited our ages and courage, and so we gradually had quite some practice. When the Danish cadets visited us, they naturally also wanted to try the 'jump-mast', but one of them did not take care. As he fell down into the net, his knees hit his chin and his mouth was severely injured. It looked terrible – so terrible that I still remember the incident and I couldn't have been more than three or four years old when it happened. The injured cadet was the future admiral and Greenland explorer George Amdrup.

We children were frightfully spoilt with toys. In one of the halls in Gatchina a real slide has been set up, where we had great fun almost every evening before it was time for bed. It was high and steep so we slid down it very speedily on small bright red mats. From time to time Father would play with us after dinner. Otherwise, there was always a Negro servant at hand, who would be more than happy to show us the ropes. Among the domestic staff there were in fact also six real Negroes. It was a tradition, which dated all the way back to the days of Catherine that there always had to be Negroes at court. They were clad in special, magnificent and colourful outfits with turbans and did service like footmen would do. Not much was asked of them, and they were not especially eager to do much, but they somehow acted as guides in the big palace, and they were especially excellent playmates for us children. Two of the Negroes, who served at Gatchina in my childhood, were 'spoils of war' from the Turkish War. One of them was a dear, old American Negro.

The best of all my friends and playmates was, however, 'Nana', Mrs. Francklin. She came to us when I was three weeks old, and she didn't leave me till 1913 when she closed her dear eyes in our house. She was nanny,

Grand Duke Michael Alexandrovich and Grand Duchess Olga Alexandrovna at the railing of the Imperial yacht Царевна (Tsarevna), *ca. 1887.*

Empress Marie Feodorovna arriving at Toldboden (the Customs House) in Copenhagen in the 1890s. Note the Cossack in the driver's seat.

teacher and friend all in one. She was the dearest and most loyal person I have ever met.

When we lived at Gatchina, which we did most of the year, a number of girls and boys would come to visit us every Sunday afternoon. They were the sons and daughters of Father's friends and comrades. We would always be thirteen children, and when we sent our friends back to St. Petersburg towards the evening, they would always be dropping with fatigue, partly because of the long way out to the palace and partly because we had spent the whole day tearing around. We thirteen children had our meals on our own, but when we were finished we were called in to say hello to Father and Mother. That would only take a moment – and then it would be time to play again. That usually took place upstairs on an empty floor, where we played hide and seek in the dark halls and corridors. I somehow think that there were some girls who were not too happy to be up there – at any rate they were always found and caught surprisingly quickly. It was, incidentally, not exactly cosy there. I remember that we had a fencing instructor, who was so frightened of being up there in the dark corridors that he always waited down below until he was called for. It was evident that he did not believe that a skill in the use of arms was of any use against ghosts.

A family reunion in the late 1880s:

Back row from the left: *Princess Marie of Orleans (married to Prince Valdemar of Denmark), Princess Louise of Denmark, (daughter of Crown Prince Frederick), Crown Prince Frederick of Denmark, Crown Princess Lovisa of Denmark, Prince Max of Baden, Princess Marie of the Hellenes, Grand Duchess Xenia Alexandrovna of Russia, Prince Albert Victor of Wales, Crown Prince Constantine of the Hellenes, Princess Victoria of Wales, Tsarevich Nicholas Alexandrovich of Russia, Princess Alexandra of the Hellenes.*

Seated in front: *Princess Thyra of Denmark, (daughter of Crown Prince Frederick), Edward, Prince of Wales (later King Edward VII), Alexandra, Princess of Wales (later Queen Alexandra), Grand Duchess Olga Alexandrovna of Russia, Empress Marie Feodorovna of Russia, Grand Duke Michael Alexandrovich of Russia, Queen Louise of Denmark, Emperor Alexander III of Russia.*

Every late summer we would either go on a trip to the Crimea or Denmark, Mother's homeland. The journey to Copenhagen was undertaken on the Imperial yacht. It was a beautiful old paddle steamer, which rolled terribly as soon as it was stormy weather – and it almost always was! In those days the trip from Kronstadt or Peterhof to Copenhagen usually took four or five days. On the *Polar Star* it only took 36 hours. The Imperial ship was escorted by several warships, but that made less of an impression on me than the fact that we had a live cow on board. It supplied us children with fresh milk, and it

Christian IX of Denmark's children 1892.
The picture was taken on the occasion of their parents' golden wedding anniversary on May 26th. From left to right: Wilhelm (King George I of the Hellenes), Dagmar (Empress Marie Feodorovna of Russia), Alexandra (Princess of Wales), Frederick (Crown Prince of Denmark), Thyra (Duchess of Cumberland), Valdemar (Prince of Denmark).

usually did its duty even though it suffered terribly from seasickness – a fate it shared with quite a number of other passengers.

When we sailed in between the old forts in front of Toldboden (the customs house in Copenhagen), a salute would be fired and soon after we would see the Royal Barge approaching. It was rowed out to us with regular strokes, and with each stroke the rowers would lift their oars straight up into the air, which gave them a nice little shower. It was highly amusing to watch. Normally, my grandfather, Christian IX, and grandmother, Queen Louise, would come out to our ship to bid us welcome to Denmark. Then we were rowed ashore and shortly after off we steamed to Fredensborg. We children really looked forward to these trips, partly because we met with numerous playmates, partly because we were treated to bread and butter with shrimps on. We didn't know that treat in Russia, and we thought it tasted wonderful. King Christian IX was the most wonderful and lovable grandfather one could wish for. He often played with us children. The Queen was also both friendly and loving, but she did not play with us – but I loved her very much all the same. As a rule, we were a crowd of children visiting 'Europe's Grandfather'. We came from Russia, England, Greece and Gmunden in Austria. There were also the Danish princes and princesses there. We were of all sizes and all ages and had such fun together all day long. And we children were all equally annoyed at being rigged out in our best clothes every evening because we had to go in to greet the grown-ups who had been invited before they sat down to dinner. We would wander around and say a polite 'Good Evening' to all the ladies and gentlemen of the court, who were standing around in the 'Garden Room'. Then Grandfather and Grandmother and the others would say 'Good Night' – and we would be packed off to bed. We were not in the slightest bit amused!

Strangely enough, I remember the time when we Russian children could always tell from the smell which children had last been in a room. The English princes smelt of fog and chimney smoke, and the Danes smelt newly washed and slightly damp. The other children claimed that we Russians smelt of highly polished leather. When I was somewhat older, I became especially fond of Prince Valdemar and Princess Marie's children. There was a year when I constantly carried little Prince Viggo around. I do not know if he liked it, but I was happy. The Queen praised me and called me 'the little mother'. That made me very proud. At times, I gave Viggo piggyback rides for hours on end – he was so tiny and so light, and I was very fond of him. Now and then, Grandmother would take me for a walk in the park and show me the flowers. She taught me how to tie a bouquet. 'Now take that flower', she would say, 'and then that one … And then the next one!' She taught me to love flowers and colours even more than I already did. Grandmother was especially fond of roses, and every morning during the last years we stayed at Bernstorff, she would walk around in her rose garden and cut off the most beautiful flowers and put them in her basket. When she came home, she would put them in small glass vases – one by one. There were flowers every-where in her rooms. Since that time, the scent of roses has always reminded me of my dear 'Amama', and I can still picture her old, gentle face.

Like other children, we had measles – and that happened at Bernstorff at a time when the Palace was packed full. We were about twenty children or even more. It was Prince Christian – the present King Christian X – who brought measles with him from the town and in the course of the next few days one after the other of us fell ill. Three of my English cousins were down with the illness in one room, my two eldest brothers and several Greek cousins

A family reunion in Fredensborg in 1903 presumably on the occasion of the 40th anniversary of Christian IX's accession to the throne:
(Prince Gustav of Denmark, Princess Dagmar of Denmark, Crown Princess Lovisa of Denmark – hidden). Back row: *Princess Louise of Schaumburg-Lippe, Crown Prince Frederick of Denmark, Queen Alexandra of England, King George I of the Hellenes, King Christian IX of Denmark, Princess Thyra of Denmark, Dowager Empress Marie Feodorovna of Russia, Prince Hans of Glucksburg, Grand Duchess Olga Alexandrovna of Russia, Prince Peter of Oldenburg, Empress Alexandra Feodorovna of Russia, Prince Nicholas of the Hellenes, Princess Victoria of Wales, Grand Duke Michael Alexandrovich of Russia (behind Emperor Nicholas II of Russia), Prince Harold of Denmark, King Edward VII of England, Princess Maud of Wales, (Prince Carl of Denmark, Princess Alexandrine of Denmark – hidden).* In front: *Prince Christian and Princess Marie Louise of Schaumburg-Lippe, Grand Duchesses Tatiana, Olga and Marie Nicholaievna of Russia..*

were laid up in another room ... and so on. I remember that Misha and I were the last to catch the illness. We had been given permission to run around and visit the patients so that we 'could quickly catch the illness ourselves'. I have the best and most amusing memories of measles. There is, however, one exception: poor Uncle Hans caught it too ... and he became seriously ill! At his age it was no joke to catch measles for the first time.

CHAPTER 2

A Train Disaster

Duties started to knock at my door during the year before my sixth birthday. I never went to school, never sat for any sort of exam and never had any classmates because, from the very first day, I was instructed by a number of very clever and renowned professors from St. Petersburg. As we normally lived in Gatchina and lessons started at 8 o'clock, the honourable scholars would have to get up early and they were quite exhausted when they arrived. It couldn't possibly have been all that amusing to travel about 100 km back and forth to teach a little girl of seven! It is with special pleasure that I remember a couple of my tutors. They are the two professors who gave me nature and history lessons. They understood that I so dearly wanted to do some of the things other children did, so they often combined their classes into two or three consecutive lessons and then we would visit museums – either the Hermitage in the Winter Palace, different public libraries or the Museum of Mining, where there were some very interesting models of shafts and the like. It was due to these tutors that I managed to see a lot. I was also allowed to accompany Mother to art exhibitions and by doing so I became interested in art in all its variations, especially painting, at an early age.

I cannot remember myself without a pencil in my hand. That was nothing special because it was something that ran in the family. My youngest brother Misha also liked drawing and always did so with his left hand. Funnily enough, my eldest boy, Tihon, draws with his left hand too. My sister Xenia also had a marked talent for drawing, but she seldom had time to do anything about it – especially after she was married and had her seven children. By the way, it wasn't that we had gained our talent for drawing from strangers. Mother had both drawn and painted during the first years after she was married in 1866. Later, it was difficult for her to find time to pursue this interest. Mother told me that when she and Father lived in the Anitchkov Palace she had to spruce herself up every morning to drive to the Winter Palace to say good morning to her parents-in-law, the Emperor and the Empress. She often had to wait for hours and when she got back there would always be two or three tutors waiting for her to instruct her in Russian language, Russian history, religion and a series of other subjects which Russia's future Empress might not be proficient in. I do not think I need to tell my mother's countrymen that she was a very wise woman, and did not need to be told what life and her position demanded of her.

One of Mother's first tutors was the lovable Ioann Yanishev, who was Confessor to the whole Imperial family and Vicar of the Court. Mother told me that when she became engaged, her fiancé had brought Father Ioann Yanishev to Fredensborg so that he could instruct her in the Russian language and the Greek Orthodox Faith. Mother was only seventeen when she was betrothed, and she was more than nervous at the thought of the Russian priest who was due to arrive to take care of her education. But Yanishev was not only a priest but also a catechist. He took Mother out sledding, and when she slid down the hills in the Fredensborg Palace Park with him he would in turn pull the sledge back up, and in that way he managed to hammer quite a few Russian words into her young impressionable brain. Mother highly appreciated this wise, mild priest, and when I too – seven years old – had him as confessor and scripture teacher, I immediately became fond of him. Father Yanishev was exceptionally popular with everyone he came into contact with and when he died there was deep mourning at the Imperial court. He passed away at a time when none of my siblings were around, and I was the only one of us who was able to follow his bier and attend his funeral.

As a rule, we children had lunch with Mother and Father. I was allowed to join them at table before I was tall enough to reach up to its edge, so I was put on a big red cushion. I always sat on Father's left side, and he was the one who cut up my food for me.

In the late summer of 1888 a tragic event took place which made a very strong impression on me. Father and Mother had been on a trip to the Caucasus together with my two eldest brothers, while the rest of us had been in the Crimea where we used to go every other summer. We had stayed with an old general, who had been 'entrusted' with us at the Livadia Palace which is beautifully situated on the Black Sea. When Father and Mother finished their tour at the end of October we were told to join them so that we could all travel back to St. Petersburg together. We met them at the agreed station in southern Russia and we were all very happy to see each other again. Then those of us who had come from the Crimea got into the Imperial train for the journey home. The first leg of the journey went well enough even though some said afterwards that they had noticed that the train had been shaking more than it normally did. The Imperial train was very heavy and drove exceptionally fast. Suddenly, the accident happened! Father and Mother were sitting in the dining car together with my siblings and the others, while I

The train crash at Borki, October 17th / 30th, 1888.

myself sat with Nana a couple of carriages further back in the train. We were sitting at a table between two windows and had a sofa on each side of us which was crammed full of luggage. There were suitcases, a bath tub and many other heavy things. I remember that I sat there waiting for the last course of my dinner, semolina, but I never got my pudding. At the very second the waiter entered our compartment disaster struck: the train started to sway from side to side. Then there was a deafening noise which was followed by a jolt. Then jolt followed jolt – one worse than the other. Nana grabbed me and held her protecting arms round me. I was terrified and could hardly see what was going on. But I got a glimpse of all the heavy cases as they tumbled down on top of us ... I felt their crushing weight ... Then my head reeled ... And then everything went black. It was impossible to breathe ... I was dead.

The Borki Cathedral was one of many churches built all over the empire to commemorate the Tsar's "miraculous" survival in the train crash at Borki near Kharkov, Ukraine.

I do not know how long it lasted, but suddenly I discovered that I could hear people screaming. Then I couldn't be quite dead yet, could I? When I came round, I found myself at the bottom of a steep slope which the carriage had rolled down. I got up onto my feet and looked back. I saw bleeding people tumbling and falling down after me ... it was

Grand Duchess Olga Alexandrovna in the late 1880s

dreadful ... and I ran as fast as my legs could carry me away from all this horror. Soon after, when the noise had quietened down, I heard fast footsteps behind me and a voice calling. It was one of the servants who wanted to take me back. He caught me, but at the very moment he lifted me up I scratched him in the face with my small sharp nails so that blood started flowing. I thought that all my loved ones had been killed and didn't want to go back to that terrible scene.

It was a dreadful disaster. Thirty-six of the royal household staff had been killed and many seriously injured. Strangely enough, not a single member of the Imperial family had been hurt. It was almost like a miracle that Father and Mother had been saved. The carriage they had been sitting in had completely collapsed so that the roof ended up lying on top of the wheels, but luckily enough the end wall right at the back had also been crushed, so when the carriage slid down the hill they had literally been slung out before the roof had fallen down. All the woodwork and every bit of glass was splintered or smashed, and the heavy iron plates were crumpled up. Father had a mark on one of his legs where his silver cigarette case had been pressed against his leg, but otherwise he was unharmed. Mother didn't have as much as a scratch on her. However, my father's dog Kamtchatca who had been lying at his feet had been killed on the spot. Fourteen to sixteen people had been sitting at my parents' table and several of them had been seriously injured. One of the ladies-in-waiting, Countess Marie Kutusov, suffered a back injury and was bedridden for over a year. Colonel Sheremetev, who had also been sitting at the table had his chest crushed, and died of this injury several years later. I can also remember that it made a very strong impression on me that the servant who had come in with the semolina pudding just as the accident happened had had his face and hands covered in it, and had been really seriously burnt.

The hours following the accident were terrible. I will never forget them. It took as long as five hours before help reached us. We had no bandages because the carriage where the first aid supplies were had been shattered and the chemist himself had been killed on the spot. The poor wounded were lying around moaning and asking for a little something to drink – but there was nothing to give them. Mother went into one of the least damaged carriages to try to find a few drops of water. There she found an old general who normally saw to my two eldest brothers' upbringing. He was lying stretched out on a sofa holding one finger in a full glass of water. When he saw Mother come he said: 'that is what Your Majesty should also do ... it is good for the nerves'. It is possible that he was right, but my mother was so furious with him for being such a egoist ... both she and Father thought more about those poor people who had been injured than about themselves. Father walked around and spread some cheer as well as he could and Mother made herself useful where there was need for her. She comforted the dying by holding their hands – they were all so fond of her. My own dear Nana who had protected me so well was among the injured. She had a big purple-blue bruise on her chin and on one cheek after my head had given her a heavy blow. I had sat hidden under that chin. She had also broken two ribs which had penetrated into her liver. I got away with a bump on the top of my head from hitting her chin.

The footman who had served in the dining car lay unharmed outside the carriage, but just as he was about to get up, the chimney fell down and fractured both his legs. Another footman was killed on the spot only a few steps from Father's seat. The poor cooks bore the brunt of so much. One was killed by the stove, and another one was scalded so badly by boiling water that he later passed away.

Finally, the relief expedition arrived. It brought doctors, nurses and first-aid supplies along, and the wounded were taken to Kharkov. However, as soon as we arrived at the first small station a priest turned up to hold a requiem to commemorate the 36 casualties … and celebrate a thanksgiving service for our rescue. After the service we all gathered for a meal together in the station building … both Father, Mother, us children, all the servants and the train staff. Everyone had a deep feeling of being brothers and sisters because we were all God's children and under his protection.

During the first days after the disaster it was rumoured that it had been an attempt on our lives and that we had all been killed. Neither was true. I heard later that the authorities had looked into the matter and found out that the accident had happened because two engines of different speeds had been coupled to the train. The one at the front had pulled more than the one at the back. That had caused a vibration which had gradually spread to the whole train and finally caused the train to derail. It took a long time for me to get over the experience. I dreamt about it for years and would wake up in the middle of the night bathed in perspiration. Still, to this day I am somewhat apprehensive about taking a seat in a train even though I have covered many hundred thousand kilometres since then without anything happening.

Countess Zinaide Mengden*: The Borki Accident
October 1888

It was on the Imperial Family's way back from an official visit to the Caucasus that the dreadful train accident happened at Borki on October 30th, 1888. The incident has so often been described that I now only want to mention that the train was derailed and that most of the carriages plunged down a steep slope and were crushed; only the Imperial carriage remained standing and that even though its walls had collapsed and the roof had caved in over the Emperor and his family, who at that moment were sitting at table and having lunch with Postjet, the Minister for Transport, and the Royal Household. To this incident I am able to add a few details, which a lady-in-waiting told me since she was present. A well-known artist had accompanied the Royals and made sketches in the Caucasus.

He too experienced the accident at Borki and made a sketch from memory of the train carriages falling down the slope. He also drew a picture of Tsar Alexander III creeping out of the collapsed carriage. Here it looks like the Tsar is lifting up the falling roof on his strong shoulders; under the picture the artist has written: There is still a God!

Source: 'The Memoirs of the Countess Zinaide Mengden'*, pages 80–81.

*Zinaide Mengden was born in St. Petersburg in 1878 as the youngest of five siblings. At that time her father was General Major in the suite of Tsar Alexander II. From 1883 till 1905 the family lived in the Tauride Palace. In 1912 Zinaide was engaged by the Empress Marie Feodorovna as lady-in-waiting and accompanied her to the Crimea and to Denmark. After the Empress' death in 1928 she moved from Hvidøre to a small flat in Venøgade in Copenhagen. She died there in 1950 and was buried in the Russian section of the Assistens Cemetery in Copenhagen.

CHAPTER 3

My Home in Gatchina

Father would always come along with us when we went away and we were thrilled to have him so close, but it was *really* best to have him at home in Gatchina. There we had him all to ourselves. We children would approach him so trustingly as we knew that he understood us and would go along with our interests. And then he knew how to get us going. When spring was in the air he would see to it that we were given different tasks which would force us out into the fresh air. We cleared the snow away and collected firewood. Together with him we would then make a lovely little bonfire where we roasted an apple or two which we later shared between us. And then there were the walks through the grounds and the deer park. From time to time he would make us look for antlers. Then he would send us off in different directions so that we would get used to moving around on our own. That could be quite frightening because the wood was dim and gloomy. A couple of times it happened that I came across a dead animal, which had already started to decompose. I didn't really like that, but I did not say anything to Father and Misha because I was after all a 'big' girl. Every single evening – it didn't matter where we were – Father would come up to the nursery to say goodnight and to make the sign of the Cross over our tired and sleepy heads. I loved that moment even though I was often only half awake, and I loved the smell of his cigarette smoke which lingered on after him when he tip-toed out of the room so as not to wake us up. That was how Father was.

Now I must say something about my two dear tutors, the Englishman, Mr. Heath, and the Swiss, Mr. Thormeyer, who lived in the Palace and were always together with us. One day we would speak French and the next day we would speak English and so on. They were very different and yet we loved them both just the same. I cannot remember when Mr. Heath came to us … he was there when I was born and he quite naturally and gradually became part of my life. However, I clearly remember the day Mr. Thormeyer arrived. I was only four years old – and he only twenty-four. He put me on one of his knees and showed me a picture book, and while he turned the pages he explained it all to me in a language I did not understand a word of. But the pictures were so beautiful and he was so friendly. Two years later, I could already both understand what he was saying and chatter away in French – and I was only six years old! Mr. Thormeyer was a born teacher and full of resources. He could play any game and make the most amusing dresses out of paper for Misha and me to dress up in when we put on a comedy or staged tableaux. He also made new dolls for our puppet-theatre and sewed new clothes for all the old ones so that they could hardly be recognized again. He was so crafty in the manner he spoke with or to us in that he also managed to make us 'invent' small plays and act them ourselves – and if we had been very good and especially diligent – he would act amusing pieces himself – while we watched him with open eyes and wide-open ears and his 'audience' would shout with joy at every single one of his many jokes. He was a proper teacher.

And then, I do not really know if he was better than our English tutor, Mr. Heath. He had white, curly hair and was very fatherly in his manner. We always called him 'Old Man', that dear soul. 'Old Man' was a sportsman in the best sense of the word. He used to say: 'A gentleman must be able to do many things – and do them well. He must be able to ride, run, fish and shoot … and on top of that he must have a clear and legible handwriting!' Oh dear, I shed many a tear when Old Man insisted that a girl should also have a beautiful and clear handwriting. He was so adamant about that point. Mr. Heath could also paint and he was a prolific artist. As soon as he had a spare moment he would grab his brushes and paint away at his many pretty watercolours. When he had finished one, he would take a few steps back to give it a critical look – and then generally tore it to pieces. They never turned out as well as he had intended them to be. I did not understand him because I thought that he painted very beautifully and I had a huge admiration for his pictures. In order to save them from sharing the fate of their predecessors I would often seize the chance to hide his watercolours before he decided to rip them to pieces. He never missed them and forgot his 'masterpieces' just as quickly as he had painted them. Later, I had them framed and hung up in my room and it happened several times that at the sight of one of his own pictures, he would exclaim: 'My dear child – who on earth has painted that lovely watercolour? It is really adorable.' When I told him that I had stolen the picture from him before he had had an opportunity to rip it to pieces he would laugh so heartedly that I had to laugh too till our eyes filled with tears.

Shakespeare was Mr. Heath's favourite author, so because of that it became my duty to read all his plays and to learn major parts of them off by heart. He had probably started putting me on this rather heavy diet too early, and even though Old Man and I made a huge effort I never really learnt to appreciate them. Several years later – I must have been 15–16 years old – a sort of amateur production of 'Hamlet' was going to be performed in the home of one of my many

*Grand Duchess Olga Alexandrovna with her French tutor, Marc-Ferdinand
Thormeyer, and her English tutor, Charles Heath, ca. 1895.*

*uncles. I would have preferred to have been excused from going, but Mother would
not hear of that. In other words, I had to go along. When we arrived at the scene
of action my Aunt looked at me with big, round eyes and started whispering to
my mother. It was clear that it was something unpleasant because Mother looked
rather uncomfortably affected. After a bit of a discussion it ended up with Mother
saying to me: 'Olga, you had better drive home again … "Hamlet" is not a piece
for young girls!' I answered that I had read it over and over again with Old Man,
but that didn't help – I was sent home all alone without getting to see 'Hamlet'.*
Before we had left home I had been distraught about having to go along, but
now that I was being sent home on my own I felt that I was being humiliated.
That is how quickly young girls' feelings can change. *When I got home, I naturally hastened to read that beastly "Hamlet" right through from beginning to
end and tried to find out what it was that was so inappropriate for a young girl
to hear about, but I could not find other flaws with it than that it bored me quite
a bit – and I already knew that. I told the whole story to 'Old Man' who laughed
so heartily that the tears rolled down his dear cheeks.*

But now I am being sidetracked. Let's go back to those happy childhood years when we still had Father with us. In winter we moved up to town where we lived at the Anitchkov Palace. It didn't have a park, only a big garden, where we went for walks every single day to get some exercise and fresh air. It was, however, rather dull to just trudge round the garden all the time so Father got the bright idea that we should build our own snow castle every winter. Father, our two teachers, Misha and I would work doggedly and were equally untiring when it came to thinking up improvements. The castle was relatively modest the first year, but our skill and ingenuity grew year by year, and the castle ended up by being both a big and impressive structure which was allowed to stay where it was till the spring sun demolished its last bastion. Every year, Father had a special medal struck for when the castle was finished and on the day we were able to hoist the flag over its walls of snow we were each presented with a commemorative medal. The last one had the inscription: 'Our work – will give the sun work'.

All children adore Christmas-time – some, I should say – perhaps most – just because it means a holiday and presents, but a few are taught to understand what Christmas stands for. My parents never missed an opportunity to remind us children what Christmas should mean to each single one of us. I still remember the feeling of awe when we children accompanied our parents through the corridors, galleries and halls of Gatchina on our way over to the annual Christmas Eve service in the Palace church. I also remember how the smell of fresh spruce lingered in the air and that it made my heart beat in blissful anticipation. The service started at half past six. In the middle of the church there was an image of the birth of Christ. It was surrounded by a profusion of flowers and when you went up to the image to kiss it you breathed in the balmy scent of hedge roses and wild lilies. Wax candles had been lit all over the church and they cast an intense but none the less subdued glow over the congregation, and when the old, but eternally new Christmas gospel was read, you were filled with a feeling that God and His angels were very close.

After the service it was time for dinner – only Father, Mother and us five children, and then the moment came, which all Danish children know, too when you sit and wait in front of a closed door and when you glue your eyes to the faint yellow strip of light which is making its way under the door till it is suddenly thrown wide open! When the double doors were opened at home in Gatchina an old church bell would be rung at the same time. It tinkled so mildly and beautifully, and then the door would be opened to all the delights. Seven Christmas trees stood around in the room – one for each of us and at the foot of each tree there was a table with presents. We already knew in advance where our personal tree stood so we would quickly run over to it – the faster, the shorter our legs were! There were, of course, presents from Father and Mother, from our siblings and the rest of the family. But there were also always boxes from our Danish grandparents and English relatives. It was one of the highlights of the festivities when the time came to unpack these boxes. As a rule, we already had a notion of what we would be giving each other, but it was so wonderfully exciting what Grandfather and Grandmother had thought of! For the next two days we were always allowed to play at the foot of our trees – then we had to pack up our things and move them up to our rooms where we shared them out among the servants who were closest to us.

On the third day of Christmas we had a Christmas party for the soldiers. It was a lovely day. On that occasion all the Cossacks, soldiers and marines, who served in the Palace, gathered for a big Christmas tree celebration. The event took place in a sort of 'manège'. Everyone present at the festivity that evening was given some sort of a practical present like for example a tea pot, spoons, knives, forks, butter dishes, porcelain plates and so on. The soldiers came forward one by one and pulled a number in a big lottery, and we children enjoyed helping each one to find the present which tied in with his number. When we found it we would run over to Mother with it with the soldier following behind us. Mother would then personally hand over the present. Everyone was also given a souvenir which was usually in the form of a spoon or a goblet and engraved with the Imperial double-eagle. The occasion lasted a couple of hours and the soldiers would trudge round the enormous Christmas tree in a never-ending procession. I enjoyed the mixture of the smell of pine and army boots – for me that was the quintessence of a *proper Christmas!*

CHAPTER 4

Anecdotes from the Imperial Court

Gatchina was the paradise of my childhood and youth. I loved being in Denmark and looked forward each time to going to the Crimea or the Caucasus, but I had never been away for long before my heart started to yearn again for Gatchina. I especially loved the spring in my dear old home. I have experienced spring in many places and under many different skies. It has always been the best time of the year for me. It is the time of miracles. As a child I saw it happen year after year in Gatchina's wonderful park and I remember those springs as the most beautiful I ever had, and the thought stirs my heart. My memory goes back to the time when I was so young that I could barely reach my Nana's knees. She would take my little hand in her soft but firm grasp and then we would go for a morning walk in the park. We started our walks each spring as soon as the first snow had melted, to see who could find the first blue anemones. They grew in those spots between the slender birch trees, where the sun had melted the snow away and made the earth soft and moist. Nana's warm, loving hand always led me to those places where the anemones grew closest together, but strangely enough, it was always me who found them first – and Nana was most surprised when I discovered a whole sea of blue anemones which was growing right in front of her feet.

Later on, Nana and I would tie bouquets of violets and lilies-of-the-valley for Papa and Mama who were such dears as to always be happy to receive them. If we went even further the big meadows would be quite full of yellow cowslips. There was no end to all the delights to be found in my paradise. Here and there in the park there were a number of pretty pavilions from a bygone age. The most picturesque and most romantic of them was situated in the middle of a lake. If you wanted to go there you either had to row out there or walk over a narrow iron bridge. It was called the Venus Pavilion. If you went inside you would find a long bench along most of the wall and in each corner there was a fountain which sent a fine, graceful splashing spray down into a marble basin. The whole ceiling was one big painting which represented Cupid in a merry frolic with a number of frivolous and scantily-clad nymphs. When you sat in the Venus Pavilion it was almost like being on a ship. From the windows you could see the entire length of the lake, and how the pale birches and dark fir trees growing on its shores were reflected in its clear water. There were several islands in the lake and numerous small, delicate bridges which connected them with the shore and with each other. It was a whole network of islands and bridges – a magic kingdom for Misha and me. We each had our own canoe and as soon as the weather was warm enough we would spend a major part of our leisure time paddling around in the lake, and playing hide-and-seek among its islands and under the many delicate bridges. How wonderful it was in Gatchina's park … it was full of idyll and so filled with melancholy … a style and a scent of a bygone age hung over it.

Father often took my brother Michael and me out for walks in the grounds and deer park at Gatchina. It amused him to show us the animals and the plants. Among the animals in the deer park we had some white deer which had been brought there from Denmark. I later met the forester, who had arranged for their transportation. We children were very fond of looking at these beautiful animals and never thought that they could be dangerous. One day, when we were out walking with Father again we heard him suddenly shout: 'Hurry up … run … in here'. We ran because Father had told us to but without knowing what the matter was. He was standing in a feeding stable and no sooner had we reached him than he slammed the door shut behind us. A split second later we heard a terrible crash. It was the white stag, who was driving its antlers into the solid planks of the door. From that day on we were more careful when we went for walks in the deer park.

We naturally had many amusing and interesting experiences, but pleasure was never allowed to take precedence over work. Anyway, I think that both Misha and I were fond of most of our subjects – with the exception of dancing lessons! A poor musician would scrape away at his violin. The dancing-master would either be raging or praising. And Misha and I would be peony-red in our faces, partly due to our efforts and partly because we were embarrassed. And that was because the frosted glass panes in the doors failed to hide us from us a group of Cossacks and sailors – fighting to get a place at the key-hole though which to peep at us.

Every autumn when we returned home from Denmark, we were one person more than when we had left. It was my Mother's old governess – Mlle de l'Escaille – who had joined us. She would then spend the winter with us and go back home to Brussels in the early summer. She was a very lively and loveable old lady and my mother appreciated her very much. Mlle de l'Escaille stayed with us at the castle and joined us on most of our excursions and trips. Misha loved to be the driver. He was good at it but often too daring and it happened several times that he would overturn the sledge in a rather too daring curve. There we would lie in a snow drift laughing and squabbling at how long it would take us to get up again. Mlle de l'Escaille was the one who laughed loudest and scolded most. As a rule, the troika would normally stop a short distance away and the horses would then turn their heads and look at us as if to say 'It is really not our fault!'

Mother had three ladies-in-waiting, who took turns to stay with us for a month or two at a time. Two of them were the elderly Countesses Marie and Aglaia Kutusov. *They were completely inseparable, came together, left together, spoke at the same time and always about the same thing and so on... We youngsters thought that they were dreadfully boring and useless, but Mother said that they were as true as gold.* On the other hand, I was really fond of Mother's third lady-in-waiting Miss Catherine Ozerova who was not so young any more either but was a very lively person. She was keenly interested in children and young people and would often take me along to a home for the disabled. Once in a while I would buy some toys or other small gifts with my savings and distribute them among her charges. She was just as happy as I was to see how delighted the children were.

Many a story was told at court about these two Countesses who were like 'conjoined twins', and who were both very absent minded and impractical. Once, when Countess Aglaia was taken ill, the eldest, Countess Marie, had to attend a diplomat's ball on her own. She was very apprehensive about going under her own steam, but there was no way out. She placed herself in the hands of her maid and hairdresser and let them see to her appearance. According to the fashion of the day, she was fitted out with huge ostrich feathers on top of her hairdo, which was done so elaborately that she was almost unrecognizable. The Countess arrived safely at the ball, let the servant take her overcoat and together with the other guests she started walking up the wide staircase which led to the ballroom. Among the guests were two of my girl friends who later told me the story. At the top of the staircase there was an enormous mirror which covered the wall from floor to ceiling. On each side of it there were doors leading into the ballroom. If the Countess had been there before, she must have forgotten the layout because she walked straight ahead towards the mirror. When she had almost reached the mirror she stopped and looked into the eyes of a lady standing right in front of her who gave her a stare. Then the Countess took a step to the right and the lady in front of her took a step to the left. The Countess then tried taking two steps to the left, which didn't help as that tease of a lady with those two crazy feathers on her head kept on following her. That annoyed the Countess so much that she lifted her lorgnette in a menace and said in a loud and irritated voice: 'Ainsi. Madame, nous ne passerons jamais!' and she was right – in that way they would never be able to pass each other! At this point a sympathetic soul took her by the arm and led her away from the mirror and into the ballroom. This is how absent minded the Countess was.

I am just remembering something that really amused us children. It is about the two Countesses K. and is supposed to have happened in the park at Peterhof. There were two fountains there – one with Adam as the central figure, and the other with Eve. They were just called 'Adam and Eve'. One lovely summer's day the two sisters arranged to meet at Eve. Aglaia arrived on time and waited patiently for her sister, but as time passed and Marie still did not turn up she finally went home. There she met Marie who had just returned from the park and was furious that Aglaia had not kept their appointment. Each one maintained that she had waited for at least half an hour at Eve. No one ever found out which of the sisters had been right. The two ladies were, of course, much too modest to turn a blind eye on whether it had been Adam or Eve they had honoured with a visit!

The two sisters had some tough hours when the Shah of Persia visited my parents. It was really funny to listen to the stories my mother told us about the old Shah's social manners. He had, of course, been brought up in the good oriental manner and had a number of habits which did not really fit in with what was customary at the Imperial court. The worst moment came when my mother had to present all the old and young aunts and ladies-in-waiting to him. He greeted the young and pretty ones with smiles but pointed his finger at the elderly and distinguished ladies and asked: 'Pourquoi ca'? He couldn't understand why the old and ugly had to be put on show at court – surely it would have been preferable to hide them away! The first time he was invited to dine at court, Mother sat next to him at dinner, and in accordance with good oriental custom he would select small tasty bits from his plate and stuff them into Mother's mouth. In return, he took those pieces from her plate which he especially fancied, so for that matter they could just as well have made do with one plate!

The Emir of Bukhara – a sort of vassal of Russia – frequently visited the Russian court. His son who was about my age was in the Cadet Corps in St. Petersburg. The Emir was an exceptionally tall and handsome man, and it was quite a picturesque sight when he and his entourage entered the hall. The Emir had a long, black full beard and wore a jewel-encrusted turban and held a scimitar. His entourage was nearly as impressive in their colourful 'dressing-gowns'. Each time the Emir came on a visit, he would bring presents – 1 day lovely carpets, another a magnificent team of horses, costly materials and much more. We still have one of the Emir's Persian carpets on the floor here at 'Knudsminde'. The Emir of Bukhara knew a little Russian, but his dignity did not allow him to make use of such a 'foreign' language which is why he always brought an interpreter along. It was a wonderfully amusing sight to see him listen to the interpreters' explanations with the greatest interest even though he had already understood everything – and even though he knew that we knew that he had already understood what had been said.

CHAPTER 5

Work and Play

I *have already mentioned my youngest brother, Michael, who we always called Misha. I have loved him since I was a baby and, gradually, as the years passed, we became fonder and fonder of each other. We have always got on well together, we played together – and never quarrelled, we had the same tastes, we liked the same people and shared every idea or thought. When he was a boy, Misha would come up to my room every morning so that we could have breakfast together. As soon as we had finished, we would go out for a brisk walk or take a ride to get our blood circulation going before the days' duties started. Lessons commenced at eight when our first tutors turned up, and continued with quite short breaks between lessons until three in the afternoon. When we were children we always had dinner in the nursery with Nana and our two 'guardians' or later our two tutors, Mr. Thormeyer and Mr. Heath. That stopped when Misha was fifteen and a half and I was twelve. I mustn't forget to mention that we were never allowed to fool around while we were eating. During the whole meal Mr. Thormeyer would often read aloud to us out of a French book, and many are the French books we got to know in this way. When it was Mr. Heath's turn to supervise the meal, he would test us in spelling from the moment we sat down till the moment we got up again. Nana often protested about this misuse of our free time and maintained that it was harmful to our digestion to eat and work at the same time, but so far I haven't noticed any ill after-effects from my two dear teachers' overwhelming energy. Personally, I was most fond of the days when we did spelling because I was better at it than Misha although I was his junior by two and a half years, and it naturally flattered my vanity.*

This nursery dinner was over by five thirty, and then Misha and I would normally go off for a ride. Nana could not ride so instead she would drive out in a barouche. She usually planned the route in such a way that she would meet us on our way home. She loved to come out in this way, see us ride and enjoy the air. Father died when I was twelve – and then all this changed. From that day on my mother wanted us downstairs to dine with her at eight, but that was no reason for Mr. Heath to compromise with his educational theories. He insisted most ardently that we should continue to take turns to carve the beef, the leg of mutton – or whatever it was so that we should know the proper way of doing so. In his

Grand Duchess Olga Alexandrovna with two friends, ca. 1887.

opinion, there was no end to what a proper gentleman and a real lady should know in order to be able to cope with any situation.

Although Nana and Mr. Heath both spent over thirty years in Russia, neither of them ever learnt to speak the language even reasonably well. They both made great efforts, but never succeeded. Their attempts at speaking Russian or trying to explain something to the servants were so incredibly funny – that we forgot all our fine manners and just screamed with laughter. Mr. Thormeyer, our Swiss tutor, was on the other hand a linguistic genius. After only a few years in Russia, he could both speak and write the language correctly.

When Misha was ten years old he was given a gun so that he could go out into the garden and practice shooting crows. I went out with him on his first hunting expedition which took a rather dramatic course. After Misha had missed a couple of crows, he hit the third one. It was, however, only injured and tried to flutter away, but fell into the lake and there the poor creature lay fighting for its life with flapping wings as it whipped the water to foam. Misha and I were equally unhappy. He got hold of a long pole and tried to pull the winged bird onto land while we both shed buckets of tears with fear and distress. Oh ... it was terrible! I never really believe that Misha ever learnt to enjoy hunting, but it was an upper class pastime, and he was the Emperor's son and 'noblesse oblige'. Mr. Heath also told him that a real gentleman had to be a good shot, and gradually Misha acquired quite a profound marksmanship even though he never became as good a marksman as Nicholas.

It was a different matter to go bear hunting – we liked that much more. The hunt usually started with a long and enjoyable sleigh ride deep into the primeval forest. We rode along on a narrow sledge to which two horses were harnessed in 'single file' – i.e. one in front of the other. Like this, it was easier for them to thread their way between the trees. It was a wonderful drive and so beautiful and quiet in the forest – so quiet that the snow laid like whole eiderdowns on the little fir trees making them resemble trolls or animals. And the horses trotted along in the soft, heavy snow almost without making a sound ... One could only hear the occasional crack of a whip and a horse's whinny ... otherwise deep silence reigned.

I remember a bear hunt where my brother had brought a tall soldier from southern Russia along. He had never before experienced a bear hunt and was so keen to see what it was like. When my brother gave him permission, he was beside himself with happiness. *We drove through the forest to the spot where the bear was known to be, left the sledge and on skies followed a huntsman further into the forest. When we came to a clearing, from where there was a good view to all sides, we were told to wait and get ourselves ready to welcome the bear. Another huntsman went on further with his two dogs (a long-haired, strong breed, which somehow reminds one of huskies), and let them loose so that they could find the bear. These clever dogs would bark and drive the clumsy big bear along in the direction of the guns. We told our friend, the soldier, that he should under all circumstances keep himself prepared as the bear would be likely to come at a good speed. While we were waiting in silence behind thick white trees and bushes, from where we had a clear view we could see him a short distance away as he stamped around and kept an intense look-out in all directions. He was literally trembling from excitement – all his nerves were strung to the utmost from this waiting. Suddenly, a small avalanche of snow fell from a branch above and catching us by the arm, he whispered: 'The bear …!' It was, however, not the bear but just a tiny bird which had disturbed one of the soft pillows of snow on its flight from branch to branch! The soldier was awfully bashful about his mistake, and of course we teased him afterwards – but not then – as an instant later the bear really did appear in the distance. We watched it plodding its way very carefully and slowly through the deep snow.*

While we were children living at home at Gatchina we often had wild animals as pets. We played with them for as long as they were small and grieved deeply when they grew so big that we had to part with them. We have had many young bears, and we brought them up on bottles of milk, honey and other delicacies. They were the dearest pets one can imagine, full of fun and play. It was, however, seldom that we were allowed to keep them for longer than about a year. By then, they would have grown so much that they would become dangerous and then we had to part with them. Most often, they continued their lives in St. Petersburg's zoological gardens. There was one of these bear cubs which we kept longer than the others. It was a female bear and we called her Mashka. She grew and became very big and strong, but she was so funny and placid that we didn't want to give her away. It was, however, necessary to tie her up outside because she was too inquisitive and wanted to visit everyone in the neighbourhood – and it was uncertain that the neighbours would have liked an unannounced visit from a bear of her size. Misha was especially fond of Mashka – as she was of him and every day they would have a wrestling match. Then they would grab each other round the waist and struggle long with each other till they finally toppled over onto the ground. Misha was not only the strongest but also the shrewdest, and it always ended with him laying Mashka on her back. One day the fight lasted especially long, and when Misha got up, he wiped the sweat from his brow and said: 'This will be the last wrestling match between Mashka and me – she is getting too strong!' The next day she had to be sent to the zoological gardens. Misha and I both cried when it was time to say good-bye and Mashka kept on turning her head towards us as if she wanted to say: 'Listen, you can't do this to an old friend!' We also felt that we could hardly do it.

There was also a time when we had a tame wolf. She was exactly like a dog in all her ways and her affection for me lasted eight years. I could take long walks with her and she was both obedient and loyal. As soon as I whistled, she would bound up to me and rub herself against me. From time to time, I would take her up to my room. She behaved as well as any dog and was as agile as a tiger. If I allowed her to jump up on my desk, she would take one enormous leap but would be careful never to knock anything down. For that matter, I would have liked to have kept her in the house, but she smelt so nasty that with all my love for her I could not keep her in the house. We decided to build a big enclosure for her down in the garden. That was her 'estate' with trees and even a river flowing through her domains. As soon as I approached the fence, she would jump straight up into the air with delight, and when I went into her she would stand on her hind legs (she was taller than I was), put her forelegs on my shoulders and lick my face in raptures. I was powerless to stop her. She was so strong that all the dogs were afraid of her and would slink away. It was a bit of a tragedy because she was as harmless as could be and always tried to make friends with the dogs, but they completely misunderstood her good intentions. That was quite a pity.

There was also a time when we had a pet squirrel. I even think that we had it for several years. The nimble little animal loved to jump up on our heads or shoulders and was very lively and affectionate. But it was also a very lucky squirrel as it had a whole little room to itself, and we fed it on nuts which it ate out of my mouth. While we are on the subject of the 'animal population', I must mention that we once had a lynx. If anything, she resembled a huge cat and she was as affectionate as a cat, but I never really trusted her. Her favourite game was also a bit too much for me. She loved playing with my knitting and she did that by ripping it into tiny pieces, and then she would roll around on the floor in a hopeless tangle of dropped stitches and threads of wool.

We always had a division of sailors, who took care of the many different boats in Gatchina's park. During the winter they naturally did not have so much to do seeing to the boats and then they had time left over to build toboggan runs. First, the sailors would make the natural hills higher by piling snow on them. Then they would pour water over them so that the whole lot froze to ice. Like this, we ended up with some wonderful toboggan runs. We would first slide down a series of hills, which had three 'floors'. From there we would fly out onto the lake and up a hill on the opposite shore, round a curve, across the lake for the second time and then half way up the first hills again. We went at such a speed down the slippery slopes that it almost took our breath away. We used to tie five or six small low sledges together so that they formed a whole train, and sit two at a time on each sledge. Then we were able to speed up. We never tired of sledding down these wonderful hills. And to make everything easier, the sailors had built steps of wood from the 'terminus' up to the starting point. It was a wonderful winter amusement and on Sundays when our young friends came to visit, our guests thoroughly enjoyed the refreshing and exciting runs on that fast icy slide.

Alexander III to Olga and Misha

Spala, 12th September 1890

My dear darlings Misha and Olga,

I thank you both a lot for your dear letters.

Today, Aunt Thyra arrived here with her eldest daughter Marie Louise. Now the whole house is full and all rooms occupied, everyone has not more than one room.

We hunt every day from morning till evening and have shot down a lot of game and wonderful deer. The weather is marvellous, it is hot and warmer than it was in summer at home, a real delight. At the manoeuvres here in the district of Wolyn it was cold, there was rain and wind, and it was only from the day of the parade that the weather improved. We saw your Bessarabian Infantry Regiment, which presented itself magnificently.

I can imagine how Mishkin is showing off without our presence at Gatchina, he probably takes charge of everything, bosses around and on the whole does what he likes and will be perfectly spoilt by the time of our return! Poor Mr. Heath [Charles Heath, 1826–1900, Olga and Misha's English tutor], *how sad and what a pity for him; we thought about him with Mama; please tell him this and give him our greetings and also to Mr. Thormeyer* [Marc-Ferdinand Thormeyer, 1858–1944, Olga and Misha's French tutor]. *Greet Nana* [Nana, 1834–1913, was Elizabeth Francklin and Olga's English nanny], *Semenov and the others. Now farewell my darlings Misha and Olga.*

I kiss you lovingly. Christ be with you

Papa

My sincere greetings to Goshi and Mme Flotow [Marie von Flotow was a lady-in-waiting to the Empress Marie Feodorovna].

Private possession

Alexander III and his family at Livadia 1893:
Back: *Tsarevich Nicholas Alexandrovich, Grand Duke George Alexandrovich,*
Grand Duchess Xenia Alexandrovna. Middle: Empress Marie Feodorovna,
Grand Duchess Olga Alexandrovna, Emperor Alexander III.
Front: *Grand Duke Michael Alexandrovich.,*

CHAPTER 6

The Last Family Celebration

In the summer of 1894, my sister Xenia was married to Grand Duke Alexander Mikhailovich. I was just about twelve years old so was not allowed to attend all the wedding festivities, but 'little pitchers have long ears' (meaning little folk or children hear what is said when you little think they do) and I both saw so much of the event and heard so much about it that I understood how it had been a most splendid occasion. A series of royal guests from other countries had been invited and the 'Fredensborg Clan' was naturally heavily represented. Among the guests was the present Danish King, whose name was then Prince Christian, our English cousins Victoria and Maud, and several of our Hellenic cousins. With my twelve years I was allowed to come along to the church. What an array of uniforms, medal ribbons and gowns there was and how the light from the heavy chandeliers and the many burning candles made the guests' bejewelled necklaces and diamond-embellished orders sparkle, like northern lights over a Siberian steppe on a clear and frosty winter's night.

The wedding took place at Peterhof. Xenia looked radiantly happy in her beautiful wedding outfit. I seem to remember that she was dressed in a silver gown with a décolleté down to her shoulders and which had a three metre long train. On her head she wore a diamond crown and from it hung a long lace veil down along her back. She was the image of happiness as she walked to the altar with her 'Sandro'. I suddenly remember that she had two long curls dangling loosely down in front onto her bare shoulders. Father ushered her into the church on his arm. There the bridegroom was waiting alone for her in the middle of the floor. My mother was very moved by the thought that she was about to 'lose' her eldest daughter, but experienced aunts consoled her by saying that she was at least able to keep her in the country.

After the ceremony there was a banquet at the Palace followed by illuminations and a special firework display in the park that evening. Unfortunately, I was too young to attend. That same evening the bridal couple drove off to a small hunting lodge, 'Ropsha', about 30 km from Peterhof, where they were going to spend the first part of their honeymoon. Quite a few people had gathered outside 'Ropsha' as they wanted to bid the newly-weds welcome. For the occasion they had equipped themselves with flares and Bengal lights, which sent one series of sparks after the other out into the dark starlit July sky. They had probably thought that it was an excellent idea, but the four horses harnessed to the newly-weds' carriage were apparently of a different opinion. They shied at the flares and the deafening cheers, and took over from the driver. And then the foursome bolted down the road in the direction of a bridge across a small river. The bridge was narrow and didn't have railings on either side. To the fright of the driver and the bridal couple, the horses suddenly made a sideways leap and disappeared over the bridge and down into the river! It looked very dangerous, and in a single moment that happy festive mood changed into one of fear and horror. Luckily enough, it ended with the newly-weds pulling well through their unintentional plunge in the water. They did indeed get quite a wetting and had swallowed some muddy water, but they were unharmed. My brother-in-law quickly got hold of his bride and carried her back to dry land – but, oh dear, in a most sorry state. Thankfully, it wasn't particularly far to the hunting lodge, and as soon as the first fright was over, they had a good laugh at the unusual start to their marriage. Our parents were not told anything about the accident that same evening, but the next morning Xenia sent her beautiful and previously white wrap and her soaked hat to Peterhof, and asked for both to be hung up to dry on Mother's fire screen so that the family could be gently prepared for what had happened. However, my parents became so anxious at the sight that I am not at all convinced that this sort of preparation was a success.

For the time being, the wedding was to be the last big family celebration in the history of the Romanov dynasty, because shortly afterwards – on the 1st of November – my dear father passed away. Who would have thought that it would have happened so quickly? Now, afterwards, we can better understand that Father had actually been ill over a longer period of time. He had already felt poorly and tired during the visit to Fredensborg the previous year, but he didn't want to frighten Mother and we children so had not said anything. His condition worsened with the coming of winter, but then Xenia was to be married and he didn't want to spoil her happiness by taking to his bed. That was how he was ... and that was why he was only ill for a relatively short time.

The last wedding guests went home, and we were again able to resume our private lives. One day, when we were out walking with Father, he told us that we would be going to Poland for some days. There we were going to stay at a brand new hunting lodge where he had never been and nor had anyone else. We travelled down there, got off at a small station at the edge of a forest and then went for a lengthy drive by horse and carriage. Finally, we arrived at the

Grand Duchess Olga Alexandrovna with the lovebirds Grand Duchess Xenia Alexandrovna and Grand Duke Alexander Michailovich (Sandro) and Emperor Nicholas II and Empress Alexandra Feodorovna ca. 1895.

new hunting lodge [Bialowieza]. It was situated on a high hill and looked wonderful. It was also beautiful inside. All the furniture and all the parquet floors were made out of different types of wood. That looked strange. And it was also strange because the furniture and the floors had not yet had time to dry out, and that made them contract every single night with enormous bangs like canon shots. I was only twelve years old, and it was a shock each time 'the furniture' fired off a new shot.

During the daytime, we would go hunting ... and there the shots continued. I, of course, didn't have a gun with me but stood post with one of my brothers. They were good shots, and I ought to have been proud, but instead I was unhappy each time they hit a deer. I can imagine that they were more than fed up with having such a little fool along with them!

It had originally been planned that the hunt should continue, but my father felt even more poorly and preferred to go to another lodge [Spala], which was also in Poland. However, that wasn't of much help. His illness continued to worsen and at Mother's suggestion we travelled on to the Crimea. She hoped that the mild, beautiful climate would help to improve Father's health. However, that turned out to be a disappointment. Fathers' health still went downhill – eventually at breakneck speed. It is sad to think about – and much too sad to write about in detail. Shortly before Father died, my brother became engaged to Princess Alix of Hesse and she arrived with the rest of us. She told me that it was twice as hard for her since she had just lost her own father … and now she had to stand at a deathbed again. A few days later it was all over.

The journey home was very touching, but at the same time very trying for all those of us, who had loved Father. The train that took him and us to Moscow had to stop at every single little station because people wanted to say their last good-byes to their Emperor. We stayed a whole week in Moscow, where my eldest brother, Nicholas, was proclaimed Emperor. He was very unhappy about having to take over such an enormous responsibility at his young age [26], and he felt the burden weighing heavily on his shoulders. Shortly after Father's funeral had taken place, Nicholas and Alix of Hesse were married. The wedding took place in the Winter Palace on my mother's birthday. We were all dressed in white court dresses, and we missed Father terribly. It was a sad wedding ceremony and a very difficult day for Mother. During the whole of the following winter the newly-weds lived with us in the Anichkov Palace, partly because Mother wanted them to do so and partly because their apartments in Tsarskoe Selo were not ready for them. It was a difficult winter to get through.

After my father's death, Mother, Misha and I went to Denmark every autumn. We stayed at Bernstorff Castle with my grandparents, King Christian IX and Queen Louise, Uncle Hans, Uncle Valdemar, Aunt Marie and their children, of whom we were always very fond. Aunt Marie had a funny donkey trap, and she would often take us children out for a ride in it. The trap was quite old, and the donkey was not of the latest vintage either, but we had lots of fun when we rumbled along the uneven roads. Then they were not like they are now. As a rule, the trip went to Ermelund, where it was difficult to find roads or paths. When you finally found them, they were mainly just stones and holes. It happened several times that the trap toppled over. When Aunt Marie realised what was about to happen, she would shout "hold tight" to Aage, Axel and Erik. She knew that I would take care of little Viggo since he was sitting on my lap. The trap was fairly low, and the donkey did not like going very fast so it usually ended up with the trap tipping its contents into a ditch, where we would land on top of each other in a squirming, laughing, tangled heap.

Grandfather loved his horses. Every single morning he would take a walk to the stables with a little bag of rye bread and each horse would be given a piece. It happened quite often that he would ask us at lunchtime if we would like to go for a drive, and we always did. The King himself would sit on the box as the driver – he was an excellent one – and Mother who was also fond of horses, and was a very accomplished horsewoman, would sit next to him. Then Grandfather would crack his whip like a real coachman and off we would go along the coastal road (Strandvejen) on a lovely late summer's day in Denmark. We children loved going for drives with Grandfather. He drove so fast and safely and knew his horses so well that he was aware of how much he could ask of them. This unerring instinct had incidentally been handed down to Mother, but it had also been Grandfather, who had originally taught her and her siblings how to handle horses when they were children.

When my grandparents had so many guests that there wasn't enough room for them all at Bernstorff, Uncle Valdemar and his family would move over to Bernstorffshøj, which wasn't far away. Often times I would slip through the park and the rose garden over to Uncle Valdemar, Aunt Marie and my young cousins, who I was – and still am – very fond of. I have many lovely memories of cosy afternoons at Bernstorffshøj, where Aunt Marie was the perfect hostess for all her guests from the oldest to the youngest, and where most of the visits ended up with us having a cup of milk and just as many open sandwiches and raspberry compote as we could tuck away. Aunt Marie would often sit and paint in her garden room. Normally, artists do not like being watched while they are at work, but I was somehow always allowed to stand next to her and I learnt a lot from that. Aunt Marie was particularly fond of painting different groups of mushrooms which we had gathered that day on our morning outing in the donkey trap. We were not allowed to prepare our harvest till she had selected the mushrooms she wanted to paint that afternoon.

From time to time, the whole family would drive over to Charlottenlund Palace to dine with the Crown Prince. Then a whole cortege of closed hansom cabs would roll up to the front door and we would be distributed in them. I still remember how they smelt of old, slightly mouldy leather. We youngsters would have liked to have had the windows opened, but that was not possible, partly because of the grown-up ladies' evening gowns, and partly – perhaps mainly – to avoid their beautiful and elaborate curls getting out of order! The evenings with the Crown Prince and Princess always started with a grand dinner.

When it was over, the party would split up. The gentlemen would go down to smoke, the ladies would sit down in a cosy corner to chat, and we youngsters would hurry as fast as our legs could carry us over to our cousins, where we played the piano, chatted and laughed so that it must have echoed throughout the house. We didn't stop till it was time to go down and gather round the tea table. After that, the evening was over and we drove home. The drive offered another exciting moment as it took us through the pitch-black Jægersborg Allé. We sat there behind the closed doors of the hansom cab, and listened to the clip-clop of the horses' hooves and the wind whistling in the tree tops.

CHAPTER 7

With Brother Georgie

As a child, my brother Georgie was just as healthy and strong as the rest of us. When he grew up he went on a prolonged voyage to the tropics and during that journey he showed signs of having been infected with tuberculosis. We found out that he had probably contracted this insidious disease from a servant who had died shortly before. When he returned home from the voyage he was, of course, immediately put under the care of a doctor. The professors, who attended to him, should most likely have sent him to Switzerland or to the Caucasus, but medical science was not as advanced then as it is now and instead they allowed him to go to Bernstorff, Denmark, where he often spat blood; and to southern France, where the damp and dusty air undoubtedly further undermined his health. It was too late before they found out that this illness is best cured in clean, clear mountain air and requires complete rest. It was then that Georgie was sent to the Caucasus.

My mother, Misha and I went, at the end of every summer, to visit my elder brother Georgie in Abbas-Touman in the Caucasus. As he was ill with tuberculosis he had to live in this small town, which lay at an altitude of 3,000 metres. The journey down there was incredibly exciting and Misha and I enjoyed every minute of it. First, we would travel for three days by train through Russia to the Black Sea. We were on the move night and day, and that was already quite an adventure. We went directly to Sevastopol where we boarded a big war ship which took us straight across the Black Sea to Batum. That voyage took another two days and two nights. That was perhaps the most interesting part of the trip because on the way we encountered huge flocks of migrating birds which were on their way south. There were birds of all sizes, from golden eagles to tiny wrens, and if the weather was bad they would at times be so tired and exhausted from the long flight across the sea that they would settle down all over the ship – sometimes even on our shoulders and heads. Hawks and starlings would settle side by side and gather strength to fly on. It was an impressive sight. *From Batum we continued by train up through the Rion valley – one of the loveliest sights I remember. At any rate, I have not seen many places, which can compete with that fertile valley. I was fascinated by the tropical plants growing in the swampy parts of it. We passed enormous tea plantations and lush orange groves on the hillsides, where the fruits lit up like drops of gold between the green foliage. Slowly we left the tropics behind us and reached the mountains. There we were rushed through tunnels and over flimsy bridges hanging across seething mountain torrents. Misha and I would run from one side of the train to the other so that we wouldn't miss anything. That day's journey offered never-ending adventures. We reached Borjom in the evening where we spent the night in the house of one of Father's uncles.*

At eight o'clock the following morning the journey continued by carriage up the steep slopes of the mountain range, with four horses abreast called a 'tchetvorka'. Later in the afternoon we reached the wild and beautiful Abbas-Touman. My brother Georgie lived with his two ADC friends and his doctor in a wooden house. We stayed in another house. His house was situated in a narrow mountain valley among steep crags which were over-grown with pine and fir trees. There was only one road to the house, and it followed a stream which trickled along through the bottom of the valley. The road continued on up over the mountain ridge via a narrow pass, which lay at an altitude of 5,000 metres. I have only been right up there once and never will I forget how beautiful it was. It was a strenuous trip, but I've never regretted it. It was incredibly beautiful up there. The sun was about to set when we reached the pass. From there we looked out over the whole mountain range – Elbrus, Kazbek etc. whose peaks were covered in perpetual snow and glowed pinkish in the setting sun. It was so quiet, so very quiet up there. The snow muffled our steps and the thin air swallowed the sound of our voices. We were all alone in that magnificent scenery and yet we were not quite alone. Two huge golden eagles glided over us and our horse – they looked as if they were not even using their wings.

Georgie's life was very monotonous and quiet so he was very happy when we visited him. Almost every day we would ride up to his house and take him along to one or other beauty spot, where we would stop for lunch. As a rule, we would have food with us in a couple of big hampers, but sometimes we even prepared it on the spot. Our favourite meal was a special type of roast lamb. It was really easy to make – we just had to put small pieces of meat on a long wooden stick and roast them over a slow fire while we poured salt water with wild onions over them from time to time. It was a sumptuous meal. On the whole, we tried numerous dishes down there which we were not used to having at home in the Palace. One of our favourites was a lovely round white cheese which was made out of ewe's milk.

Life in Abbas-Touman was just as young people like it. It was primitive and healthy and romantic at the same time. The place was not all that far

Grand Duke Michael Alexandrovich, Grand Duke George Alexandrovich,
Empress Marie Feodorovna and Grand Duchess Olga Alexandrovna, 1896.

from the Turkish border and there were quite a few robbers in the area at that time. To be on the safe side we always had one or two Cossacks with us when we rode off on lengthy trips. When we went for walks up in the mountains with my mother, an local man would always accompany us at a distance. *I must add that our escort was always armed, but there is really no need to mention this as every man and boy in the Caucasus is always armed.* It varied a little as to who would escort Mother and the rest of us. Mother did, however, have a 'favourite bodyguard'. He was a young Caucasian with a calm, handsome face and strangely fiery eyes. His name was Omar, and Mother often chatted with him as she enjoyed listening to what he told her about the lives and conditions of the local population. Mother teased him and would ask him with a smile: 'Omar, when I look into your eyes, I am sure that you were once a robber'. He would shake his handsome head and smile back. Mother continued her teasing several times in the course of the summer. The autumn was coming to an end and it was time to return to Gatchina and St. Petersburg. On one of our last days in Abbas-Touman we went for a walk up in the mountains. Omar followed us. When we stopped to look down and admire the view he suddenly stepped right up to us. He was quite pale with emotion and stammered with agitation: 'Come,' he said to Mother, 'I want to tell you something!' And then he told her that he had really been a robber in his early youth. That was a long time ago, and he asked her to forgive him. Mother was very touched by his honesty, and by his courage and trust. He had placed his life in her hands … it would only have taken her one word and he would've been hanged. Mother naturally didn't say anything … she kept his secret and he became our most loyal and dearest protector for as long we came to Abbas-Touman. In 1899 our dear, gentle, patient and good Georgie passed away from us. He was 27 years old and I had just turned 16. Since then, we have never been back to Abbas-Touman. None of us wanted to see the place again. Incidentally, both Georgie's aides-de-camp and friends died too of consumption at a young age. They had cared so loyally for him and had paid for their friendship with their lives.

For a while after Georgie's death we naturally didn't go anywhere, but we had to get on with life and gradually we started to socialise again. I was now about 16–17 years old and at that age Mother had to take me along to balls. It was the custom that a young girl should 'go out and enjoy herself'. But whether it amused me was quite a different matter! I was ready to burst into tears every time I had to go to a ball and be with people who I did not know and who I did not want to know. Mother often had to speak seriously with

Grand Duke George Alexandrovich and Grand Duchess Olga Alexandrovna, ca. 1898.

me to make me go, but that wasn't of much help! I was equally unhappy each time. I do not think that I was especially fun to have along at balls because I was not particularly fond of dancing and was probably rather shy. But for all that the balls of my youth brought me one great pleasure. It was customary to be given lots of flowers when you went to a ball. When I received some especially lovely bouquets, words could not describe how I looked forward to coming home with them, and as soon as I could in all decency get away I would leave and drive home with my precious booty in my arms. Then, when I came up to my room, I would set about putting the flowers in water. Before I'd left home, I would've made sure that all my vases were on the table and filled with water and then I would go round and distribute my dear flowers in them. I would never go to bed before each single one was put in water, and it has happened many a time that the first pale light of dawn had started to colour the horizon before I was quite finished, and could settle down for the night.

CHAPTER 8

My First Marriage

My sister Xenia often came to stay with us in Gatchina bringing her husband and young children along – they would always come at Christmastime and then again for the whole spring. When we went to Peterhof, they would come with us and stay with her father-in-law, the old Grand Duke Michael. His summer palace was situated on the Gulf of Finland, not far from Peterhof. It was a very big and spacious building in the middle of a pretty park. The old Grand Duke Michael was Queen Alexandrine's grandfather. The Grand Duke had six sons and one daughter, Anastasia, and the six brothers adored their sister – and later her daughter Alexandrine. I first met Denmark's future queen in 1894, when she visited her grandfather. She was an exceptionally pretty girl of fourteen. Alexandrine was adored by her uncles, and they were very proud of their beautiful niece. They spoilt her dreadfully and gave her one present more gorgeous than the other; she was an exceptionally lovely girl.

I was by now about seventeen or eighteen years old, and I was so happy when my young nephews and nieces came to visit us at Gatchina. We often played on the old slide where I, too, had had many wonderful times as a child. The slide was still the same, the fun was the same – and the Negroes were also the same. They had just grown a little older and become somewhat more grey-haired, but they were still just as obliging and happy to be allowed to 'play along' like they used to do when I was little. When Xenia and her children stayed at Gatchina, I would wolf down my dinner and rush up to the nurseries to help give the whole flock of children a bath – one after the other – it was a great joy to see how they gradually started recognizing me. Then they would be given their gruel and milk, and finally, after they had been tucked up in bed, I was allowed to hear them in their evening prayers. A moment later they would be sound asleep with their little round cheeks pressed deep down into the soft pillows. Another day was over.

When I was 18 I became engaged to a prince of Oldenburg (the branch of the family, which had settled permanently in Russia), and in the summer of 1901 we were married in Gatchina. As a child, I had always dreaded the thought of marrying a foreigner who would take me away to his own country, where

Grand Duchess Olga Alexandrovna on the day of her wedding to Prince Peter of Oldenburg, July 27th, 1901. Grand Duke Alexander Michailovich (Sandro) in the middle escorting them in the courtyard of Gatchina Palace.

I possibly would not thrive and where I would always pine for my beloved mother country. Now it made me happy that I could always live in Russia, and would never have to live in a foreign country. My mother-in-law had a huge estate south of Moscow. My husband wanted to live in the area, so we bought an old house in the neighbourhood which we did up nicely and then moved into. We always spent the autumn there. The estate was so far out in the country that I had ample opportunity to come into close contact with the peasants. I visited them in their small ramshackle huts, became godmother to their children and did my humble best to help the old and the sick. During those years I learnt so much from these dear simple people. I learnt to admire their touching patience and their unwavering faith in God – qualities which made them so rich in their poverty.

There was also a hospital on the estate, where two exceptionally consci-entious doctors worked with the greatest self-sacrifice and love for their calling and their patients. The hospital was fairly large – it was so big that the four nurses there had more than enough to do, so it wasn't in the slightest bit strange that I was to be found there almost every single day. I liked being

Grand Duchess Olga Alexandrovna and her first husband,
Prince Peter of Oldenburg, 1905.

there and would read to the patients or chat with them. At especially busy times I would also go along to the operating theatre and do what I could do in the place of a nurse. I learnt a lot from these visits – things that I would have much use of later in life. So few people understand that it isn't enough to learn while one is still young. Throughout life we humans must learn from everything we see and everything we experience, and try to find out how we can make use of what we learn for the benefit and pleasure of both ourselves and others.

Our house – or estate if you like – was called Ramon. It was a white building in Empire-style with supporting pillars, and was situated on the top of a high steep hill which the horses did not take kindly to. On the other hand, we were pleased with the location because we lived on 'dry' land. In Russia the spring arrives all of a sudden, and the masses of snow melt in a very short

Grand Duchess Xenia Alexandrovna and Grand Duke Alexander Michailovich (Sandro) with their children 1909–1910: From left to right: *Prince Nikita, Princess Irina, Prince Andrei, Prince Dmitri, Grand Duchess Xenia with Prince Vassili, Prince Fyodor and Grand Duke Alexander with Prince Rostislav.*

time. That makes the rivers overflow their banks and flood the lower lying parts of the country. When we arrived at the closest train station in the spring, we were not met by a horse-drawn carriage but by a boat. First, we had to row ourselves clear of the wood, which stretched its biggest crowns up over the surface of the water in a most strange way. Later, we reached the country road. We could not see it, but we knew that it was there, because we rowed along the telegraph poles whose tops and bells stuck up out of the water. It was a strange and very interesting trip. When we had rowed a couple of kilometres, we could see the house's white façade shining through the pale green leaves of the oak trees. It was always a new experience to row through a three kilometre stretch of water. Round the house there was a gorgeous old garden, which stretched all the way down to a small river, the Voronez.

The view from the house stretched over kilometres of woodlands and meadows. The wood changed colour with the season and always had a new and surprising hue. The river wound itself gently and quietly through the meadow, and whispered intimately here and there to the age-old willows which bowed their crowns and were mirrored in the clear trickling water. We were really far out in the country. The closest sign of the 20th century's dizzy pace was hidden behind the fringe of the wood three kilometres away. It was a small, insignificant railway station with a staff of a couple of men. At this focus point of civilization the one great event of the day would happen – a train would arrive and unload a meagre bag of mail onto the platform. In the spring, the mail would then have to be rowed further out to the recipients. This didn't speed up delivery, but we managed all the same. As a rule, the floods lasted for just under a month, and for as long as there was enough water we would go out in our boat every single day. Often we would row far into the wood among the tree tops which stuck up over the water like islands. From time to time, we would notice that we had rowed straight into a submerged bush which wasn't big enough to get its head out of the water. It was at the same time delightful, amusing and exciting. After a good fortnight the water would start to recede. From day to day you could measure on the trees and telegraph poles how much it had sunk, and start to talk about when it would disappear altogether. And then, one fine day, the water would be gone and we were again 'farmers'. The time which followed the flood, was wonderfully beautiful. As soon as the water receded the flowers would start emerging out of the rich, moist earth and the huge meadows would be transformed into enormous, vast and multi-coloured flower parks. They would be covered by a strange and pretty profusion of flowers, with rare plants which are normally only to be found in especially well-tended gardens. There was a riot of colour and a scent which would almost take your breath away. Every single meadow was an enormous flower bed which you would never tire of exploring.

Our house was situated between two rivers. The Voronez flowed on one side of it – and the Don on the other. The Voronez would lap up earth from our garden every year. The Don was 20 km away, and a wide and fertile steppe stretched between the river and the house. The two rivers run almost parallel for the last 100 km, when the Don swallows up our little Voronez and spreads out just like a snake after it has devoured its prey, without having been able to digest it properly. The area we lived in was very beautiful and interesting. In the good old days, Peter the Great had built his ships almost on the spot where our house was situated, and let them float down to the Black Sea via the Voronez and the Don. When we were out picking flowers in the spring, it often happened that we would find large wooden pegs and the like which had once been used for building ships.

Ramon was, of course, somewhat isolated, but we lived in a beautiful place and our house was always full of friends and guests who came to enjoy the quiet life in the country, and to go hunting or riding. However, not all our guests understood how to appreciate the joys of the country. Once, one of my very best friends, a young girl of about my own age, who still lives with her parents in Paris, came to visit me and see Russia. I very much looked forward to her coming, and to showing her the neighbourhood. She came – and we threw our arms round each other's neck with joy. She thought the house was delightful and that the garden was enchanting – and everything went exceedingly well – for one day! Then when she heard that there were 40 km to the closest town, she was struck with horror. To cheer her up, we took her the following day to the most beautiful view we had in the whole area. What did she do? She just sat down on a tree stump with her back to the view. Apparently, it didn't mean anything to her.

The next day we asked her if she would like to join us for an exciting evening walk in the primeval forest, where she could hear the wolves howling. That appealed to her very much and off we went after sunset. There were four of us in the party, my present husband with one of his fellow officers and us two.

I must remember to say that wolf hunting is only permitted in Russia in the late autumn, but the huntsmen go out into the forest in the late summer to find out how many wolves there are in a pack. They do that when the parent wolves are out hunting and the cubs are left at home on their own. The huntsmen then start howling in the same way as the adult wolves do when they call their cubs close. We had done this so often before and always enjoyed it. Well, we set out shortly after sunset and drove to the forest. At the agreed spot we met our old huntsman and friend, Theophan. We jumped down from the carriage, tethered the horses to a tree and stole our way quietly into the darkness. When Theophan got to a spot which he thought was suitable, he started howling like a wolf. That made my girl friend start and she became even quieter than she had already been. Theophan howled again – a forbidding, drawn-out howl, but still there was no answer. He howled again and again and suddenly we heard a wolf's faint little voice answer in the distance – it was almost like a dog yelping. Shortly after, the other cubs responded too … and a few minutes later we heard furtive steps in the darkness around us. Now they were quite close. We could see their eyes shine in the dark, and could easily count that there must be about five or six cubs. My girl friend gripped my hand so tightly that it almost hurt. Suddenly, she grabbed my arm and whispered: 'Now it is enough … Let's go home … this is not in the least bit funny!' Well … it had been for her sake that we had set out so there was, of course, nothing else to do than to return home. We found the carriage, clambered into the seats, said goodnight to Theophan and told the horse to trot home. It was a pitch-dark night and as such, it's best to let the horse find its way between the trees. It's much better at doing that than we are.

I needn't add that this little pleasure trip did not give my friend the enjoyment we had hoped for. She left shortly afterwards. Since then, she has often visited me in St. Petersburg and Peterhof, but has refused to come again to the countryside. It was such a disappointment for me!

CHAPTER 9

I believe in Miracles

We lived in quite an isolated spot – the nearest sizable town was 40 km away. That town was called Voronez after the river it had been built on and which flowed by just outside our garden. The river had not only lent its name to the town but had brought both trade and prosperity to it. Voronez was quite an ordinary Russian town like so many others, and had several upper and lower secondary and grammar schools, a large agricultural college, a very old monastery and a garrison which consisted of two cavalry regiments.

A hundred km away there was a considerably smaller town with a very, very old, very beautiful and artistically very important monastery. The town and monastery were both situated high above the River Don, and from far away you could see the white walls of the monastery and the golden domes of the churches gleaming in the sunshine. Inside the monastery stood the coffin of St. Tihon. He had once been the bishop in that region, and had been greatly venerated by his whole congregation. He had been canonized after his death and his memory was respected and revered throughout Russia. This resulted in an enormous annual pilgrimage to his monastery. People of all ages and from all levels of society would flock there to celebrate his name day. It was an unforgettable sight. They came in thousands from all parts of the country. Somewhere down in the Caucasus a peasant and his wife decided that they, and their children, would undertake the journey to be present on St. Tihon's name day. They dressed in their best clothes and set out. Just outside their town they met a couple who were also on their way up there, so they decided to travel together. By evening the two couples had probably become a hundred. At night they would lie down by the roadside and sleep with the sky as their blanket. The pilgrimage to St. Tihon took place in August, and at that time of the year it is always very hot and dry in Russia. When day started to break they would get up, have breakfast and continue walking. The hundreds would gradually grow into thousands and the thousands into tens of thousands. It was an impressive and colourful procession. From the colours and designs of the pilgrims' dress, one could immediately see where each one had come from. New groups would join them, and in the end the sound of the singing would rise to the heavens like an organ peal which could be heard far and wide. When you encountered such a crowd of pilgrims, you had the feeling that the whole of Russia was underway.

Do I believe in miracles? Yes, I most certainly do. I have seen them happen with my own eyes and have experienced them in my own life. In the summer of 1903 my brother, the Emperor Nicholas, had to attend a major church festival in the South of Russia, and he asked the family if any of us wanted to join him. I did, of course, very much want to. The occasion for the festival was that a deceased and highly venerated priest, St. Seraphim, who had been the region's spiritual advisor for nearly 75 years, was to be moved to another cathedral. For years people from all over Russia had collected money to give St. Serafim a handsome new coffin. His name was known far and wide, as was his goodness and kindness to all in sorrow and need. He had lived and died in the monastery of Sarov. Much has been written about his life and good deeds, and many were the people who used to leave his cell comforted and happy, cured of their illnesses and with gratitude in the hearts. After St. Seraphim's death there was great mourning in Russia, and people visited his grave and continued to crave his help, and received it.

When it became known that his earthly remains were to be moved to a different and larger church, it is no wonder that an enormous crowd found its way to the monastery to take part in the church festival. This festival to celebrate the moving of Seraphim's sarcophagus was yet another proof of the love and faith people had in him, and his help. The multitude that came to Sarov was so enormous that it was quite impossible to even think of providing the pilgrims with a roof over their heads. Thankfully, it was hot and dry weather, so that they could spend the nights in the fields and by the roadsides. It was an impressive multitude but at the same time a sad one. They came from all corners of the country, bringing with them incurable cripples and the mentally deranged, just like people had once come to Christ himself and thronged at his feet expecting to be cured and imploring for a miracle. Great was their faith. Never before had I seen such cripples as were being brought to Sarov. I saw a child … I don't know how old it was, but the body resembled that of a two-year-old, and on that little underdeveloped body there was a head twice the size of the whole body. The child was strapped into a home-made wooden cart on small wooden wheels, and had been pulled all the way there by its parents from the very northern regions of Russia. There was another man – with two paralysed legs. He had dragged himself along the sandy roads for many hundred kilometres. He had turned on his side and worked his way along with his arms and hands. What faith these peasants had.

My brother and those of us who were with him stayed at the monastery. The Emperor had a room at his disposal which was otherwise reserved for the bishop and the rest of us were put up in a series of guest rooms which were plain, but clean and cosy. *From the window of the room we slept in, one looked* out over a large wide meadow by a small river. This space was covered by all the pilgrims, and it was there that most of them slept or just knelt in prayer all through the night to be ready at daybreak to enter the cathedral, and other numerous churches, for mass. It was a touching sight indeed, and one never to be forgotten. During our stay in Sarov we also had the opportunity to see the cell where St. Seraphim had lived in winter, and go into the forest to see the tiny wooden hut which the Holy Father had built with his own hands. It was there that he had lived in the summer when he chopped wood for the monastery, and was alone with his God. We also saw the huge stone in the forest which he had knelt on to pray for 40 days. By now, it was many years since Seraphim had died, but it was not further back in time than there were still people alive who could remember him. We met an old woman, who was getting on for 80 and who had known the Saint when he used to visit her parents. She had much to tell, but alas – there was not time enough to hear as much as we would have liked to. I have since read the life works of the Saint written down by her father. For three days we felt so elated and happy in these surroundings, and free from the burdens of everyday life. My sister-in-law, her sister and I bathed in the river by moonlight because the other pilgrims did so.

I remember one day when we were all on foot going along a path by the river. There was, of course, a crowd doing the same. I remember having noticed a peasant woman and her son. She was holding him round the waist as he clung to a branch with both arms over his face. I glanced at his legs as I passed and saw that they were as thin and wasted as sticks – they were paralyzed. I then noticed that the mother was holding a small kettle in one hand. Half an hour later as we returned the same way we saw a commotion in the crowd. Some were singing, others were falling on their knees and praying. I recognized the old peasant woman. Tears of joy were running down her wrinkled cheeks – her son was standing by her side. She began to tell us that she had fetched water from the well of St. Seraphim and had poured it over her son's legs and feet praying the while – and oh what joy – suddenly he began to stretch them out little by little until they touched the earth – and there he was standing next to her and was cured! I think we felt just as happy as did the old mother. Many of the pilgrims began telling us of other cases of miracles and there were many of them, but for me who had seen how the paralyzed son had been cured, none of them were incredible. I had seen how God had rewarded true faith.

Then came the evening before the consecration in the big cathedral. Thousands and thousands of pilgrims were let in by one door, passed by the new coffin and came out on the other side. This went on all the evening and through the night.

The sights one saw were exactly what one reads about in the New Testament. There were people possessed by evil spirits who screamed and struggled as best as they could because they did not want to go into the church, and who would fall on the threshold foaming at the mouth. But as soon as they were inside the church and stood at Seraphim's coffin they would calm down, and the evil spirit which had shaken them so severely would leave them. These poor people who were now cured from this awful illness passed through the church and could go back to their homes – perfectly well again. I also remember a girl who could not speak. In the church her mother prayed so intensely for her child while she wrung her hands till the knuckles turned white – and suddenly we heard the girl scream 'Mother, Mother' – she could speak again, and the happy mother pressed her child to her heart and wept for joy. St. Seraphim was so near – one felt his presence ... and everyone praised the Lord's name.

Since then, I have often felt that life would have been much easier if one had always been able to retain the feeling of happiness that filled us in those unforgettable days.

CHAPTER 10

Initiative and Determination

*M*y father-in-law, Prince Alexander of Oldenburg, was an outstanding personality and an indefatigable worker for the community. His head was
always full of ideas for the good of the public. He built pleasure grounds like
Tivoli, theatres, schools, hospitals, cheap eating-houses and what not for the people
in St. Petersburg. Prince Alexander was not only terribly exacting of the people
who worked for him, but also demanded a lot of himself and never compromised.
God have mercy on those people who in one way or the other tried to pull the wool
over his eyes or stab him in the back. He could be terrible in his wrath. No one
who had once felt the thunderbolt of his rage would ever want to be exposed to it
again. Among the many buildings which my father-in-law was involved in con-
structing were the Institute for Experimental Medicine and the Serum Institute.
He personally knew both Pasteur and Ehrlich and all the great men of his time. His
frequent travels around Europe were partly to visit them, and partly to become
acquainted with the latest improvements or discoveries in the field of medicine
that he had heard about, and that he wanted to bring home for the benefit of the
public.

My father-in-law started this useful welfare work in his youth, and he carried
on tirelessly till the end of the war when he was over 70. He enjoyed popular
recognition for his great intellect and impressive initiative, and accepted numerous
honorary tasks. Among other things, my father-in-law was entrusted with the lead-
ership of the expedition which was sent out to deal with all the epidemic diseases
that had broken out on the border with Asia, both the pest, cholera and the like. I
remember another characteristic instance of his love of mankind and energy. At the
outbreak of the war in 1914, he saw to it that huge cauldrons with boiling water
were placed at _every single station_ so that the troops could drink hot tea if they
needed it. It was a most popular arrangement, and I am in no doubt that it
helped to curb the many throat complaints and other ailments that flourish up
during war time.

During the winter my father-in-law lived in St. Petersburg and as soon as he
was at home he would keep 'open house', and anybody who wished to speak with
him could come at 12. Afterwards, everyone without exception would be asked to
stay for lunch. It was a most unusual group of people that gathered round his

table. For instance, a minister, a doctor – who had asked for help or advice – and an editor would be there. Then perhaps an unknown actress who sought his patronage, a professor or a shy little workman who had been sent for to explain one or the other detail in the scenery department of the theatre, which at that moment interested my father-in-law. We never sat down to lunch less than 18–20 persons. I am sure it must have been most difficult for the cook who never knew in advance how many mouths he had to feed.

My father-in-law was a brilliant host with a surprising insight into a long row of fields. He was a master at starting and carrying on a discussion so that every-one at the table was drawn into it and participated. Many a time I would sit there and marvel at the energy and brains of this old man, who seemed to know everything and could talk and discuss anything, and make people feel at home and comfortable in perfectly unaccustomed surroundings. My father-in-law naturally had some funny sides which he himself was the first to laugh at. For instance, he always wore a small black scull-cap which he had the habit of endlessly twiddling round and round on his head when he got excited. That often amused me. My father-in-law had the most wonderful sense of humour and a catching laugh which was impossible to resist – and yet most people were dreadfully frightened of him. That probably had something to do with him being hot-tempered if he came up against narrow-mindedness or ill-will.

One of my father-in-law's great ideas was that Russia should have her own Riviera. He found a small town on the East coast of the Black Sea in the most uninhabited part of the Caucasus, called Gagry, which he wanted to convert to Russia's Riviera. It undoubtedly had many of the qualifications which were needed to become a popular tourist resort. The climate there was ideal and so were the surroundings, but the only means of getting there was by boat. He always said that it was ridiculous for Russian society to go abroad when there were lovely places all over their own country which they might as well visit and enjoy at much less expense, but no one wanted to go there; it was the fashion to go abroad and that was the end of it – for the time being at any rate. I have been there myself over and over again – and once under quite dramatic circumstances: my father-in-law who normally enjoyed good health, and had an enormous capacity for work, had been taken dangerously ill so it was deemed necessary to send for us. The journey down there was not at all straightforward. Even though there was a road along the coast it was impossible to get to Gagry overland, as there were no bridges over so many of the wide rivers and ravines. That meant that we had to go by boat and that was quite a lengthy and cumbersome journey. Happily for us, the crossing went quite well as the sea was more or less calm; but when we approached Gagry it became evident that it was impossible for the steamer to moor so strange, prim-itive boats with Turkish rowers came out to fetch us some way from land. We jumped down into them and were rowed towards the shore. It was impossible to row the last bit so we had to let our boats be carried in by the waves. Finally, the boats and their frightened contents were thrown up onto the pebbly beach.

Gagry was extremely primitive and indeed not the place to be taken ill in. We had brought a doctor along with us, and his one and only thought was to move my father-in-law back to civilization as soon as possible where there would be a better chance of taking precautions if the illness was to take a turn for the worse. It was, however, impossible to move him at the beginning, so we had to stay and make the best of it. It was a strange picture which unfolded before our eyes. A huge hotel was under construction at the foot of a mountain, but it was not yet ready to receive guests so we all lived in small huts built into the old walls of an ancient fortress right down by the beach. The work on the hotel and other buildings was, however, well underway so there was quite a number of workmen around. They lived in three different colonies, one for the Russians, one for the Turks and one for the Persians. Next to our abode there was a hospital for them in a round tent. While we waited for my father-in-law to get well enough to be moved, we went for walks and had a look at the area. I especially enjoyed going to the different work camps and watching the men preparing their different types of food. When the Turks bake bread they roll the dough out quite flat and then throw it against the inside wall of their oven where it turns into something like 'kuga-bread' – dry and hard; it had a good taste too.

At last, my father-in-law's temperature fell so much that he was feeling stronger and the doctor insisted on taking him home. That was easier said than done. Firstly, one could never be sure when a ship would be passing, then one had to signal for it to stop and lastly it was no easy undertaking with an ill man who was too weak to walk, and who had to be carried into an open boat and pushed out to sea At long last we succeeded in getting a steamer to venture up to the vicinity of Gagry. Then the worst part of the expedition started. We first had to get the patient out to the steamer. He was carried on board a small boat and we accompanied him. The day was warm, but the waves were high so our Turkish rowers jumped into the water next to the boat, and pushed it out to sea through the breakwaters. We were drenched a couple of times and feared that the boat would capsize, but the Turks managed to right it. As soon as we had got through the foaming surf, they jumped back into the boat and rowed it safely out to the passenger steamer where they succeeded in carrying my father-in-law on board, albeit with some difficulty. I mustn't forget to mention that the rest of the journey home went well and that my father-in-law recovered relatively quickly from his serious illness.

This first visit to Gagry took place in 1902, and on that occasion I did not get a very good impression of the place and had difficulties understanding my father-in-law's enthusiasm and sharing his optimistic belief in its future as an international seaside resort. Since then, I have visited Gagry twice and I must admit that I have somewhat changed my opinion. When I was there last I saw that the place had changed into quite a modern seaside resort, thanks to the enormous energy of my father-in-law, and was then up to the standard of the best I have visited in other places in Europe. The climate is ideal and the surroundings wonderfully beautiful. For me, there was also a great attraction there and that was nature. I have eaten my fill of wild strawberries at the end of February. The hillsides were a mass of orange and yellow as one drove by – azaleas growing wild and lovely under cypress trees and tangled briars.

For as long as we had to travel to Gagry by sea it was a difficult journey, but it didn't take long before my energetic father-in-law took the initiative to improve the country road to Gagry. After big, elegant iron bridges had been built over the mountain torrents and ravines we could drive all the way there from Novorossisk by motorcar. It was a memorable drive, and I enjoyed every moment of it though it took us nearly two whole days. The road was very smooth and good and the views changed all the time. You would drive up the mountain and see the sea far below, then the road would wind itself round deep ravines, over high iron bridges, through thick woods where the undergrowth was thick with yellow sweet smelling azaleas and suddenly you would be driving downhill again, passing small settlements where there were orange groves, vineyards and where buffaloes were lying in a river with only their dark heads and horns showing above the surface of the water. From the constant turning and twisting of the road some people not only felt but were violently sick. This looked so funny! At every bend of the road we would look out for the sight of the head of police of the district we were passing through. Poor man – he thought it was his duty to accompany us in his motorcar and drove in solitary glory in front.

The area all around Gagry was mainly uninhabited – there were but two or three families there and they had three young boys. We found out that they had never thought of christening these young gentlemen and while I was there I was asked to be godmother. Father-in-law had, of course, found the walls of an ancient church and restored it – so there was a priest there too. The boys were brought by their loving parents and were dressed in the Caucasian national costume, including daggers. Now, in our church – as one is christened under water – it took me a long time to undress the lads, pull off their high boots and unfasten the daggers. At last, they were ready, and the three young 'adams' walked in front of me to the font. I know they did not enjoy the part when they were lifted one by one and immersed in the water. One even set up a howl. It again took a long time to dress these young warriors, but the parents came to my rescue and finally we could sit them round a breakfast table, which was much more to the taste of the newly baptized Christians who showed good appetites and smiles.

The more often I came to Gagry, the more beautiful I found the place and its surroundings. We would go on excursions and find interesting ruins here and there – small fortresses and remains of Greek-Catholic churches and the ruins of castles surrounded by high walls. These castles stood high up on cliffs and we used to climb up to them and wander about. Once and only once I found a remarkable black orchid growing from these ruins. It was just like velvet and I had never seen the like of it before or after. Of course, I painted its portrait and sent it to my botany professor, who was most interested and found its' name – but I have forgotten it. Christmas roses grew about in abundance – pink, white and dark pink ones. There were also masses of cyclamens growing in the clefts of rocks and filling the air with their lovely scent. All these plants grew in winter time – but at Gagry it was like hot summer. One winter, we picked several kilos of lovely wild flowers in the mountains and valleys around Gagry, and I brought them safely back to St. Petersburg despite the frost and cold on the way. After they had been doctored at a florist's I used them for a ball I gave for the cotillion. Everybody was delighted – many had never before seen these Caucasian flowers. They were a great success and a cheap one into the bargain.

The population of the Caucasus is so varied and there are so many different tribes – each one speaking a different language and each one wearing a different national costume. Who would ever believe that not far from Gagry there is a small settlement of real coal-black Negroes? They had been there so long that they did not know when they had settled down there or where they had come from. Somewhere else there is a tribe which stems from the time of the Crusaders and where the men wear armour (côte de mailles). For an unknown reason their ancestors had not wished to return home by the customary route through the Balkans, but had instead tried to push north round the Black Sea. There the unexpected high mountains of the Caucasus must have frustrated their plans and to this day many of the descendants of these Crusaders – though typical Caucasians – have blue eyes and fair hair and live a life of their own up in the mountains among their sheep and goats.

CHAPTER II

At the Imperial Palace

A difference of fourteen years between siblings is so great that you don't, at first, mean anything to each other. It is only when the younger child has passed through childhood and teenage years that you begin to matter to one another.

That was the case with my eldest brother and I. In my childhood I remember only little of him – a big boy dressed in a sailor's suit who would walk past me once in a while; then a young officer who was very sunburnt when he came home from camp on rare occasions in the summer.

One year, my parents went on a cruise in the Finnish Archipelago. They loved to have a two to three week holiday in mid-summer. I was alone at home in Peterhof with my inseparable Nana, and my eldest brother was alone in a nearby camp with his regiment. One Sunday morning he took his young sister along to a service in the small palace chapel. I remember it so clearly. It was a very hot morning, the air was oppressively sultry and a storm was brewing. It was so hot that the church door stood open during the whole service to let in some fresh air. There had been bright sunshine from early morning and the sun had beaten down in such a strangely ominous manner. During the service it had slowly hidden itself behind some very heavy clouds. I was not really happy about the situation because I have always been afraid of noise and pandemonium – and especially of thunderstorms! At any second I expected the lightning to flash and the thunder to rumble with those horrible claps which always made me jump. I somehow think that the manner in which I cuddled up to my brother showed him that I was not yet that terribly big and sensible, but he did not say anything. Suddenly, the storm broke loose, but it did so in a very different manner than I had expected. Without any sort of warning, and without the slightest sound, a big ball of fire flew in through the open door. It floated slowly round the church and finally attached itself under a big chandelier which hung from the ceiling. All eyes were turned towards this ball of lightning which looked alarming and menacing. Most cheeks were pale and we expected an explosion at any minute. The cantor stopped short in the middle of a verse. The only person who was seemingly unconcerned by the situation was the priest, Father Yanishev. He continued

The Imperial Family 1905
Back: *Grand Duchess Tatiana Nicholaievna, Empress Alexandra Feodorovna*
with Grand Duke Tsarevich Alexis, Emperor Nicholas II,
Grand Duchess Olga Nicholaievna.
Front: *Grand Duchess Maria Nicholaievna and Grand Duchess Anastasia Nicholaievna.*

the service as if nothing had happened, and without looking at the strange ball of fire. Suddenly, it loosened itself from the metal tip of the chandelier and glided out of the church just as slowly as it had previously drifted in, and disappeared from sight. How long did it last? Perhaps some minutes, perhaps just a few seconds, but so much had happened in those exciting minutes.

It was as if that strange happening had tied me closer to my brother. The years passed. I had grown up. He had become Emperor. We were both married. The difference between my eldest brother and his youngest sister was gone. I loved being with him and was very fond of my sister-in-law, and when they had children – five lovely ones in all – I gave them all my love. Strangely enough, there was less age difference between my brother's eldest daughter Olga and me, than between her father and me. That amused us very much and he was very fond of calling me 'my eldest daughter' when he drove out with five girls. My poor sister-in-law – the Empress – was seldom able to join us. She suffered from a serious heart disorder so it was seldom that she was able to participate in parades and celebrations. When she was unwell, they sent for me – someone had to be there to ensure that the children behaved properly, stood up when necessary and greeted people as they should – and anything else there was to look out for. In the end, it was taken for granted that I always had to come along wherever they went.

I was very fond of all my brother's children but perhaps most of the eldest, Olga. The two of us were soul mates. She resembled me in character, and that was perhaps why we understood each other so well. It often happened that I was able to tell her how she was thinking in one or the other specific situation, and that always took her by surprise. 'How do you know that?' she would ask with blushing cheeks. I would then laugh and tell her that it was because I knew that she was thinking along the same lines as I did myself, and that was why I could read her thoughts.

My nieces did not have any playmates, but they had each other, and prob-ably did not miss them. All the same, I think I can say that they were awfully pleased when I visited them and brought some change into their daily lives. What a lot of fun we had each Saturday. It was then that I went out to Tsarskoe Selo for the whole day and where my brother, the Emperor, and his family lived during the winter. I took the train from St. Petersburg to the station there, where I was met by a sledge and taken for two kilometres through the streets of the town, and along the lovely avenue of larches. *The sledge would slide silently along the hard snowy road up to the white gates and then drive up to the large white palace. The first thing I did was to run upstairs to the nursery where I generally found Olga and Tatiana finishing their last lesson before lunch. They had professors and tutors who came from town to instruct them – just as ours used to do in the old days. If I arrived before the professors had finished the morning's work, they would be just as delighted to be interrupted as I had once been. At 1 o'clock we would rush down the narrow wooden staircase leading from the nursery to their mother's room. We generally found my sister-in-law on her sofa working on Christmas presents. She knitted and sewed beautifully and made many things for friends, the poor and for bazaars. Her daughters knitted and sewed beautifully too, and were never allowed to sit and idle their time away.*

Generally, it took quite a while till my brother joined us. There were so many people he had to receive every day, and so much for him to read, that he could not be punctual for meals. We, naturally, waited for him and at the self-same second he arrived we would go over to the table, or sooner said the table would come to us. It had been laid in an anti-chamber and was carried in by two footmen. We then all sat down for lunch. No time was wasted. It varied somewhat how many people were there for lunch, but as a rule it was only a narrow circle. Sometimes we were 'only the family'. At other times, the old minister of the court, Hofmarshall Baron Fredericks, would join us. It also happened that my brother asked the adjutant, who was on duty that day (they changed every 24 hours) to have lunch with us. Directly after lunch my brother would hurry off to his work, new meetings and more people he had to receive. That lasted till about 3. In the meantime, the rest of us would sit and chat and sew. When he came back, he, the children and I would go for a good quick hour's brisk walk to get some fresh air. Sometimes we skied, but the trees grew so close on all the hills so that was not really much fun. The children preferred to walk and so did I. There was always much hilarity when we returned home and had to change our boots and clothes before tea. It was almost a tradition that I had to be knocked off my feet when I stood on one leg ... and my nieces would roar with laughter when I fell onto the floor. The worst came when we descended the narrow staircase ... As soon as I started to walk down, someone would always put out the light so that it was impossible to see a thing in front of you. In the meantime, someone else would lie down on one of the steps and when I trod on her she would grab me by the ankle and tickle me or think of other tricks. There was much laughter and screaming as we all rolled down to the bottom of the stairs in a heap – knocking our heads against the banister on the way. As you fall lightly when you are young we always reached the bottom safely, or more or less without a scratch. This was how we appeared at the tea table every Saturday afternoon, happy, laughing and squabbling about all the dreadful things 'the others' had thought of. We had hearty appetites for the bread, butter, honey and milk which awaited us. It is true that it was called 'afternoon tea', but we all disliked tea.

It often crossed my mind that it must be strange for my nephew, the little heir to the throne, Alexis, to watch us big girls romping around with so much hilarity. He was the youngest of the whole flock and could not join in. Ever since his birth he had suffered from a dangerous bleeding illness, which made it quite impossible for him to play so happily with the rest of us. His life would be at stake if he even got a single minute scratch. Alexis was such a dear, and endured his illness with admirable patience. He looked well and healthy so no one who saw that handsome and high-spirited boy could imagine that he suffered from a life-threatening illness.

Every afternoon at 6 o'clock we would drive over to the church for evensong. As a rule, there were six or seven of us in the same sledge which naturally gave cause for more fun. The church lay in the middle of the park, and the service was open to all the Cossacks and soldiers who wanted to attend. The church was always full to the last place and the calm, bearded and rugged faces of the Cossacks and soldiers were so lovely in the flickering candlelight. Their deep voices were most beautiful. After the service we would drive home, have dinner, put the children to bed and have a pleasant time chatting till 11 o'clock when the train took me back to St. Petersburg. We had such lovely and happy days together, and when I got back to my room I was very content and very tired.

Olga Alexandrovna to her niece Maria Nicholaievna

1914

My darling Maria!

Thank you for your good and nice letter. The backs of my legs are very tired so I am lying on the bed and writing to you – waiting for supper – it is already about 9 o'clock. There has just been a wonderfully touching vespers in one of the wards, where the light casualties are, and it was so touching to be in the middle of a crowd of wounded praying Christ-loving soldiers – who have already spilt their blood for their Tsar and Motherland – such dear creatures! Those who could, stood – others sat, and those who couldn't were lying down.

This reminded me of our lovely Saturdays of last year and this one in Tsarskoe and the vespers in the lovely cathedral – and here there were only soldiers, who sang all on their own, and a wounded patient, who joined in as he sat on a stool next to me just in his underwear.

I do not know what else I can say to you. We all do the same day in and day out, and I do not know what to write about. T.A seems to have written to you all while she knelt on the window-sill, like I am doing now. We hardly have any chairs – and they are not necessary – we only sit at the table for meals since during the daytime we are not at home, and if we are at home, we lie down on the bed to give our legs a rest. Greetings to Shura, Lisa and Nyta. I kiss you all my dear darlings. The Lord be with you. I love you, your Aunt Olga.

Source: GARF (Russian State Archives, Moscow)

CHAPTER 12

The Army Manoeuvre

It was a shame that I did not know the whole of my native country, and that I have only been to a few places. Perhaps it was because the country was so big, or perhaps it was because life tied me to those places where we always stayed, or there was just not enough time to travel around. There was really so much to see. It was my dear tutor, the historian Platonov, who showed me all the museums at that time and who so much wanted to take me to a number of ancient Russian towns, so that we could visit the old churches together. Unfortunately, I didn't get to go anywhere with him. Later, when I was grown-up, it was difficult to find time to travel, because we had so many other things to attend to. Russia is, of course, so big that it is almost impossible to get to know the whole country. I have, at any rate, had to content myself with small, modest bits and I have seen enough to confirm that Russia is not a country in the Danish sense of the word, but – as already mentioned – 'a giant who cools his forehead in the Arctic Ocean while he bathes his feet in the tropical air of the Mediterranean'.

All the same, it happened in 1903 that I had the opportunity to accompany my eldest brother to Pskov, where the big autumn manoeuvres took place. Pskov was one of the towns with a past, and I had always wanted to go there. On this occasion I had the pleasure of seeing many of the most lovely old monasteries, churches and buildings dating back to the 12th and 13th centuries. We lived in my brother's private train all the time and it was just as comfortable as if we had been at home. Each of us had a small compartment. He also had a carriage which had been converted into a study. Further, the train had a dining car where we would meet for meals. It did not pull up at the station but in a delightful pine forest a short distance from town. After breakfast we would ride out to watch the manoeuvres which were interesting, even though I did not understand much about it all from a military point of view. I remember that it often rained during the first few days, and that we were soaked to the skin by the time we returned home for lunch. It was quite a task to get out of our wet clothes which stuck to our bodies. We welcomed the opportunity to experience some of the hardships of a soldier's life, and I enjoyed the trips' adventures including the daily 'shower'.

In the afternoons, we would go on shorter or longer trips into the beautiful woods. I often went with my sister-in-law. One day we found a spot where the ground was completely covered with the most wonderfully blue gentians, which I had never before seen growing in the wild. They were exceptionally lovely, and my sister-in-law and I were so happy when we picked these dark blue pretty flowers and were able to fill all the vases in our 'train hotel' with them. We also went out to pick blueberries. There were so incredibly many of the sweet, juicy berries that one could literally stand still on one spot and eat your fill. On one of the first days my sister-in-law had an accident. She tripped and fell, and was so unlucky as to break an arm. That meant that she could no longer ride out with the rest of us. It was sad for her – mainly perhaps because she had to sit idle without being able to work on her beloved, inseparable, needlework. She was adamant that the rest of us should go out without considering her and her arm.

On other days we would go to the town of Pskov to see some of the churches from the 12th and 13th centuries. They were magnificent with their thick walls, painted interiors in the Byzantine style, and their very high domes which were held up by supporting pillars like gigantic altar candles. The light of day and the beams of sunshine could only penetrate into the church through the narrow windows in the old thick walls, but the heat of the day could not force its way in. It was so dark when you went into the church that you could not see anything until your eyes had adjusted themselves. Then, when you left the church, you were almost blinded by the daylight and the bright sunshine.

We also visited an interesting and quite big exhibition of local handicraft. The most beautiful monastery I have ever seen was the Petchersk Monastery. We went out there in horse-drawn carriages, and the outing lasted the whole day because there were so many interesting things to see there. In the old days this monastery had been a fortress. If its thick walls could talk they would be able to tell us about Polish and Swedish sieges. This was why the thick walls made the monastery look like a true fortress from the Middle Ages. To get into the monastery you had to drive through the archway in the thick wall, which was more like a tunnel than a gateway. There were many churches inside the walls – both on the ground and under it. They differed a lot in shape and colour. We were, of course, met by a group of local church dignitaries which was headed by the bishop. He arranged for us to see the whole monastery from the highest watch-tower to the deepest catacomb. We were accompanied by an archaeologist who told us a little about the building's historical significance and mentioned some dates, but I was so busy looking at all the unusual and beautiful things around me that I did not take it all in. All that comes to mind is there was once a monk named Mark, who found a cave in the red sandstone in 1473, and settled down there as a hermit. Other hermits joined him there and in due course, these devout men started digging a church down into the ground with their own hands. Gradually, at a depth of seven metres, they dug out the whole of the big church with the thirteen pillars which held it all together. From this church you can walk through narrow corridors to other churches, which are all in the Byzantine style with old painted walls. It was pitch-black down there and we slowly groped our way along the corridors holding wax candles. On the way, we came across a number of coffins containing the earthly remains of the monks who had created this remarkable complex of buildings. It was all very interesting. When we came up and went outside again, and the wind blew out our little wax candles, we had the feeling that we had been carried back several hundred years in time – like in a dream – and had suddenly been called back to a new life.

On most days we rode out in the early morning to watch the big manoeuvres. If we had decided one evening to be present we would be off whether it was pouring rain or glaring sunshine. Perhaps the most interesting incident I experienced was the crossing of the river Velikaya. On the way, my brother's adjutant told me that the task was particularly difficult because the current was so strong, and the riverbed conditions so bad. When we arrived at the river, the engineer troops had already started building a pontoon bridge over it. It was clear that it was a difficult task because each time a soldier waded into the river and was thrown off his feet, he had great difficulties finding a foothold again on the slippery stones which covered the river bed. The engineers persevered without heeding the triviality that they were drenched to the skin, and shortly afterwards the first infantry regiment could storm over the bridge, while the cavalry had to wade through the river. It was all very exciting and impressive.

On the last day of the manoeuvres we stood on the top of a high hill from where we had a magnificent view of the whole neighbourhood. It was very interesting to see how the soldiers, dressed in their summer uniforms of white linen tops were approaching the hill from two sides. Suddenly the signal was given to storm forward and the soldiers appeared on all sides. It was as if they would clash in an enormous scuffle, but just before the two forces established contact with each other, my brother gave the order to his two Cossacks to blow 'stop', and the signal was immediately repeated by all the other buglers who were participating in the exercise. The sound travelled like an echo over the whole region making all those thousands of people stop in their tracks.

The manoeuvres had lasted for seven days, and had now come to an end. *Immediately afterwards a luncheon was served for all the officers. A tent had been raised in the middle of the square and it was here that the most distinguished guests had their meal. The hundreds of other guests were seated at long narrow tables outside. When my brother and sister-in-law walked to their carriage after lunch, the whole crowd of officers closed round them to cheer and to see them off! Many of the younger officers had never before had the opportunity of seeing them and accompanied them all the way to their carriage. I tried to follow as I was supposed to return with my brother and sister-in-law, but got brushed aside and completely squashed in this dense crowd. I could not recognize a single face as they were all from the Warsaw district. I was beginning to feel quite alone and aban-doned, but then suddenly I felt an arm stealing round my waist. A dear friend, General Derfelden, looked astonished into my face and asked: 'What are you doing in this crowd?' Well, he got me out at last, but by that time the carriage with my brother and sister-in-law was long out of sight. With some difficulty and delay another carriage was found and I was sent back to our train. Do you think that my brother was sorry? Not at all! He laughed and said: 'Oh, so it seems that we forgot you in the crowd!'*

In summer, we all lived in Peterhof – not together but each family in its own villa or estate. My eldest brother and sister-in-law lived quite close to us. Their home was right down by the water and had originally been a square tower, but several wings and annexes had been added to it as the family had gradually grown. My brother and sister-in-law lived in the tower and the children in the new extensions. Many of these summer residences were typical old Russian-style stately homes like, for example, Oranienbaum, where Aunt Catherine – Father's aunt – lived. She had her summer residence in her so-called Chinese Palace. It was a strange long building in the Chinese style, and all the rooms inside were also in the Chinese style. Perhaps they were very elegant and precious and it was fun going there – just like it is fun to visit a museum, but it was not especially cosy. Then there was an uncle – my mother-in-law's brother – who lived in a big, high building in the Tudor style. It was, however, only Tudor, when you saw it from the front because on the other side it was in the Pompeian style with small tiled courtyards, trickling fountains, formal flowerbeds and marble statuettes. My mother-in-law's house was called 'The Farm' and it had in fact been built round a cowshed. If you hadn't known that in advance you would have been able to smell your way to it because there was a smell of cows all over the house. My mother-in-law had intentionally had her summer villa built like that as it was said at the time, that the smell of cows was very good for people suffering from consumption.

When my brother was out on his morning walk, he would almost always make a point of calling on Mother when she was having morning coffee. I did that too quite often, but I always came in a horse-drawn carriage because I then lived quite a way away – about six kilometres. My mother wanted her children to look in on her every single day, and that is what we did. One day, it was for morning tea and another day it was for lunch at 1 o'clock; at times she would phone and ask me come in the afternoon and then accompany her to visit an elderly uncle or aunt who was spending the summer in the area around Peterhof.

CHAPTER 13

A Handful of Travel Recollections

I *have never really been fond of travelling and always felt very distressed when I had to leave home to go abroad, yet I had to – there was nothing to be done about it. When I really had to travel, I preferred to go to Denmark where I always felt comfortable, but otherwise I have not been to very many places. Once we went to Norway in 1909 on the yacht 'Polar Star'. The fjord up to Christiania, which was what Oslo was called then, is a lovely sight and reminded me quite a bit of Finland, only, of course, that the Norwegian cliffs were much higher and became mountains before we got to the end of our journey.*

My maternal aunt, Queen Alexandra, arrived on her yacht the 'Victoria and Albert' on the same day as we did. She came with her daughter Victoria whom we all loved, and we were often together. We had a lovely time sailing into Bygdø every day where the King and Queen lived, and it was good to have some time with our relatives. Otherwise, we went for long drives or walks to see more of the country – often in the company of the officers from the two yachts. Now – after so many years – I remember Holmenkollen best. We had an enjoyable lunch there one day and a lovely walk down the mountainside through the beautiful woodlands.

I have only been once in England and that not for long. All the same, the remarkably pretty gardens and woods filled with spring flowers left an ever-lasting impression on me. However, I did not like London itself. I have also been to Paris – that is a place I really dislike. I know very well that I am calling down everyone's wrath over my head when I say this, but I really do not like Paris in the slightest. Everyone should be permitted to have a personal opinion and be allowed to say what he or she thinks. Fancy how tiresome life would be if everyone loved the same person or the same place! The very first time I was in Paris was when I was just 20. That was when my first husband was having health problems and we were sent to the Bay of Biscay, where we stayed in Biarritz. The journey there went through Paris. I remember how those of my girl friends who were of my own age and who had never crossed Russia's borders before were green with envy and said, 'you lucky devil, how lovely for you that you will see Paris.' There were so many who said that so in the end I began to think that it was perhaps true that I was lucky, but this was soon over. We arrived in this wonderful town on a rainy, cold evening in January. The hotel we stopped at, the Hôtel Mirabeau, which had been much recommended by elderly aunts and uncles, turned out to be an old-fashioned dump that stank of gas and had a narrow wooden staircase which made me shudder at the thought of what could happen if a fire broke out … it was altogether a horrible place.

Biarritz was, however, wonderful. We stayed at the Hôtel du Palais which was situated right down by the beach. Nothing was more attractive than standing by the windows and watching the enormous waves during a storm, and seeing how they rolled in from the Bay of Biscay till they were finally crushed to cascades of water and foam on the concrete jetty. They were as big as a three-storied house – if not bigger. We witnessed several storms that winter and during one of them our hotel burnt to the ground, and that even though it stood right down by the sea where it should have been relatively easy for the firemen to fetch water.

The fire had broken out up in one of the servants' rooms, where the wind had blown a burning lump of coal out of the fireplace and set fire to the carpet. It was half past five in the afternoon of that stormy day when the fire was first noticed. We could just about see it from our windows on the ground floor. At first, we were all told that it was a triviality and would be over in a few minutes and that there was nothing to really worry about. Half an hour later the flames had, however, spread so much that we began to understand the seriousness of the situation and at last the whole top storey was aflame, and a man rushed along all the corridors ringing a bell and shouting that everyone should get out as soon as possible. A panic ensued. Doors opened and banged, ladies shrieked and ran wildly about; some were already in hysterics.

This was exciting, and I ran upstairs and administered glasses of water to some English ladies and suggested that I help them pack their things. Meanwhile, my maid had dragged the sheets off our beds and emptied the contents of our cupboards into them while all our boxes and part of our clothes were burning up in the loft. Thus, with each one of us grasping a huge bundle we staggered out into the darkness under clouds of hot smoke and rains of sparks, and crossed the garden and street to a hotel opposite. From its windows we could see our poor Hôtel du Palais burning down. The storm was so violent that not only did it carry sparks with it but whole burning beams which it hurled against the walls of our refuge. … It was a bad night! … When I was about to go to bed I noticed that I had something small in my tightly clasped left hand. I opened it to see what it was that I had wanted to 'save' so much. It was a small piece of wood that we had used to put between the sill and the window to prevent it from rattling. This is how I behaved during my first fire!

Although the fire was a serious matter – especially because a whole scale panic had almost broken out – we were convinced that it had its positive sides because we made many friends during and after the fire. They brought life into our stay. We made new friends – both Spanish and French – and were invited out to hunts, balls and picnics with them. They showed us all the pretty places in the area and took us to San Sebastian. We even saw a bull fight. This sight made me sick for two days and I shall never ever want to see another one – thank goodness.

To thank everyone for their kindness to us we arranged a small ball and invited everyone we knew. Perhaps this was a kind of mistake which I found out later. It seemed that in our eagerness to reciprocate so much hospitality we had invited so many of the 'wrong people, who one should not invite'. Well – anyhow, we hired a villa for the afternoon with a big room to dance in and a long veranda outside where others who did not care for dancing could sit, have tea and chat in the meantime. It was a really jolly event and one felt that people amused themselves well. As far as I was concerned it was somewhat of a doubtful pleasure – and that for the following reason: just before coming to Biarritz I had had to cut my hair off short and as it was then not 'a la mode' to go about short-haired I wore a really nice wig and hoped that nobody would notice it! Just as I was dancing in that jolly crowd a couple came bouncing along and gave me such a knock in the back that to my horror I felt my wig jump off and fall to my feet. Bending down quickly I caught it and tried to put it on, but alas I put it on all wrong so that it would not fit ... Feeling sick from shyness and despair, I tried to get out of the crowd and discovered that not only was my wig crooked and twisted – but that my cotillion ribbons must have slipped down over my head when I had bent down, and they were now hanging across my face under the wig!!! There was nothing to be done but to pull the damned thing off again – oh, what an embarrassment in front of all my guests and to have to leave the ballroom to arrange myself properly in front of a mirror in the corridor. I thought I would die with shame – being so very young and stupid. My cavalier had fled, and from the fright of it all I shall never know or remember who I had danced with. When I returned my knees trembled – but as I was at once invited to dance again my miserable state of mind soon cleared.

Twice we went to Karlsbad. My brother Misha and Nana went with us so we enjoyed it immensely and drove daily to all sorts of sights and heights, where we got the best coffee I have ever tasted. After Karlsbad we went to Italy. How we loved it! We went straight to the Bay of Naples and stayed in Sorrento at the cosy and old-fashioned Hotel Tramontana for over six weeks and enjoyed every minute. We donned our bathing costumes in the morning and spent the whole day in and by the water. We would sail along the coast, jump into the sea and swim ashore to see new places. Then we would dry ourselves in the sun and get back for lunch much to Nana's relief. She had waited patiently for us on the terrace overlooking the bay and listened smilingly to our happy accounts of our swimming exploits. One day, our old tutor, Mr. Thormeyer, came all the way from his home in Geneva to join our party and stayed till we were due to leave. There was so much to remember and talk about.

Of an evening, after the heat had fallen, Misha and I would get all the children in the hotel together – about 18 of them. We would romp madly around with them and teach them all the games we ourselves had loved to play in our childhood. We had some wonderful evenings and it didn't take long till the children pestered us every day for more games. With the swimming all day and the playing with the children in the evenings Misha and I felt that we just 'had to stay at home'; so there wasn't much time to go on excursions further a field. We were, however persuaded three times to leave Sorrento – once to climb Mount Vesuvius and twice to visit Pompeii. Both places were thrilling and interesting in the extreme.

Before we went to Mount Vesuvius I was told at the hotel that I should buy a pair of strong mountain boots as whatever I would be wearing that day would be ruined and could never be worn again. I did not quite understand how this could be as I had climbed many a mountain in the Caucasus and my shoes had never been ruined. However, I listened to this piece of friendly advice and bought a pair of strong boots – very cheaply – and we started out. For the first bit we went by funicular and then we continued on foot. It got warmer and warmer as we climbed round the mountain until one could feel the heat coming through the ground – there were cracks here and there and someone said that if you put an egg in one it would be hard-boiled almost immediately. As we hadn't brought an egg with us, we could not try out the experiment. At last we got to the top and could look down into the huge crater. A bubbling sound could be heard, and steam ascended snake-like from the depth and filled our nostrils with the smell of sulphur. The edge of the crater which we were standing on was about one metre wide – one was as careful as possible not to fall into it. Turning round, one had the loveliest view of the whole Neapolitan Bay and could see the isle of Procida (also a volcano) in the blue distance. The ascent had taken us just over an hour. When we thought it was time to return from whence we had come by funicular, two guides caught each of us under both arms and literally rushed us straight down that steep, grey-coloured, dusty mountainside. I thought it great fun and so did Misha, but I am not sure if the rest of the party enjoyed this long and precipitous run! It was perfectly true about the footwear! When we got down there was hardly a bit left of my new purchases. They had been cut and torn to shreds in those burning hot grey ashes and on those sharp bits of lava.

Pompeii made the deepest impression on me, but what can I relate about the place? People have said all there is to say about Pompeii – one enters it through a stone archway and on either side along the ancient stone wall one is rather astonished to see large iron rings – like those one sees on piers to fasten boats to. As Pompeii lies high above the sea one ponders over the fact of those boat-rings – until the guide tells you that the sea once came right up to this wall! On entering through the archway one finds oneself in the small museum where one sees plaster casts of people and even of a poor dog. They had all been caught and suffocated by the rain of burning ashes and boiling water that destroyed that luxurious town and all its inhabitants. As I stared at the forms that had once been alive I felt the horror of their deaths, the anguish the people must have felt, and with these feelings still haunting my mind I started to walk along the long empty streets. I looked at the remains of temples, a lot of marble statues, vases and utensils that had been dug up and placed here and there. There was but one perfectly restored house – the Casa Vecchio – with its little garden-yard, its marble fountain and painted walls, and my thoughts went back to the people and the day when Mount Vesuvius erupted and put an end to all their gay lives in such a terrible way. One still sees the ruts deep in the stone streets made by the cartwheels so many hundreds of years ago. I had read several books about Pompeii, but the impression of our two visits there left me with something much deeper and stronger – I could feel and imagine it all. We were told that the nearby town of Herculanum was even more interesting. It had been destroyed by flowing lava, but we could not get there – alas! – there was no time.

And then we went to Rome. From the very first morning we went out to see the old part of the city, I felt as if I had come 'home' to something I had always known and loved. We hardly saw anything of the new Rome, but preferred to trudge around in the old part. It was like reading the New Testament and seeing the places with one's own eyes. Over the years so many holy things had been brought over from Jerusalem to Rome so that a walk around town was just going through the life of Christ. There was for example the pillar to which our Saviour had been tied when the Roman soldiers mocked him, and the 'Scala Santa' or stairs up which he had been led to be tried by Pilate, and many other things. On our first day we twice met our servants who were also out looking at the old city. They were bare-headed and reverently crossed themselves each time their guide showed them one of these memorials from the early days of Christianity. One of our footmen was a Catholic and also very devout – he had tears in his eyes when he thought of the early Christian martyrs and their sufferings in the Colosseum and how they had been killed in the arena by wild animals. We were all so impressed by what we saw, and by all the feelings those places brought back to us, that we saw nothing at all of the new town of Rome. Apart from the Vatican, everything else felt small and held no interest for us. No, St. Peter's was anything but small – and also left an impression of greatness – but in quite another way, of course.

CHAPTER 14

My Brother Misha

(*Michael Alexandrovich, Misha, was born in 1878 and was a few years* older than Olga. They were very close as children. He was Tsarevich between 1899 and 1904 until Nicholas II and Alexandra had a son. He married, morganatically, the twice divorced Natalia Sergheevna Shermetievsky in 1912 which led to his estrangement from his family and hence postings to Orel and with the Caucasian Regiment. He was assassinated by the Bolsheviks in the Perm area in 1918, along with his faithful secretary, Johnson. His body has never been found).

*I*n 1904 Misha joined the Imperial Cuirassier Regiment, which had its old his-*torical barracks just opposite the park and palace of Gatchina. We knew the regiment well as my mother was its honorary Colonel-in-Chief, and the Cuirassiers did guard duty at the palace. Ever since Misha was in the regiment, we naturally had another tie to it and made many new and loyal friends among the officers. Some of them used to join us on our daily riding trips and would spend their Sunday afternoons and evenings with us. As soon as the weather permitted it, we would go off for picnics, which Mama and we all enjoyed. This was how I met the young lieutenant Kulikovsky, who is now my husband.*

There were so many lovely places to go to even if rain was expected, and then there was a lovely, old derelict farm in the middle of a big garden, which was surrounded by fields and woods. It was our favourite spot, because there was something to do there for everyone. You could go for long walks or fish in the big lake after the evening meal. I was so fond of picking wood strawberries, which I made compote out of for dinner. In the neighbourhood I found the most beautiful wild pansies in many different colours. They would last for weeks in vases at home. One of my mother's lady-friends, who normally came along on these picnics, was an expert at making potato salad. She had an especially 'spicy' recipe, which I never learnt to follow, but where chopped onions played a major role. Her potato salad tasted wonderful– which all 'picnic food' normally does.

It was, however, often Misha and I that did the cooking. We liked doing that. We had learnt the art from our friend Maksimov, who was our mother's chef, and

Grand Duchess Olga Alexandrovna and Grand Duke Michael Alexandrovich., ca. 1910.

who had somehow always found time to teach us. I must say a few things about him as he wasn't just an ordinary man or chef, but also an artist with a talented personality, and he was very intelligent. Maksimov spoke many different languages. He had even learnt to speak Danish like a native Copenhagener. He accompanied Mother on the 'Polar Star' when she went to Denmark and did the cooking on the way. During the time she stayed at Hvidøre, she wanted proper Danish food, which her father's old Danish chef, Witting took care of. That made her really feel at home. Then Maksimov would have a holiday and what did he do? He had earned well, he did not save his money, but rented a lovely furnished villa on the coast and engaged a cook to prepare his meals … and then he enjoyed life immensely as he was now the master of the house. When Misha and I stood bent over the pots and pans at our 'summer estate', we sent Maksimov many a friendly thought as did many of our friends there.

We never grew tired of going out to the old, abandoned farm, which was so full of poetry. The house was of wood and painted yellow. It had massive white pillars and a small balcony at the top. On each side of the house there were glass verandas from where there was a wonderful view of the garden and meadow. The window frames had wooden carvings, which were painted white. The atmosphere took you back a hundred years in time. We wouldn't have been surprised to have seen a procession of ladies and gentlemen from Napoleonic times come walking through the door, and down the stone steps. We all adored the house, but personally I was even fonder of the garden. Misha and I loved to wander around in the old overgrown garden where the grass was full of harebells and humming bees. There was also a path there, which was overgrown with grass and where you could walk on its soft green carpet under ancient oaks and yellow acacias along an old wall

Grand Duke Michael Alexandrovich in a military camp, ca. 1910.

of rough stones. You could see the fields on the other side of the wall. The path led to a gate and beyond it was an avenue of huge mountain ash trees. It was there that Misha and I sat one late summer evening looking at the setting sun, which made the mountain ash berries glow twice as red. We sat there without saying a word while we nipped off blades of grass and listened to how one of Misha's friends – a lieutenant, who we were both fond of – told us delightedly about his coming marriage to 'her', whom he had loved since his boyhood, but who had not wanted to wait for him and had married someone else. Now she was free and ready to be his wife. He was so happy, but alas for him he did not know that the marriage would bring him much sorrow. They were wed, but she ruined his life and trampled on his heart three years later. Since then, mountain ash trees with the setting sun shining on their red berries always remind me of that summer evening of so many years ago, when we were so delighted with our friend's happiness.

The Cuirassier Regiment had an annual gala day. It was held on the 9th of May and we started looking forward to the day's events long in advance. The celebrations always started with a grand parade in the palace courtyard. On this occasion the regiment would, of course, be lined up in full dress. It was an impressive sight to see the six hundred tall, white-clad figures in their golden helmets and shiny gleaming cuirasses sitting on their fiery reddish horses like pillars of stone. This parade was a joy from our earliest childhood. Every year we would sit on the window sills, listen to the band and watch the event. We did not have any lessons that morning as our masters were eager to see it all too, and as the years went by Misha and our friends were there as well and took part in this grand spectacle. After the parade we all went to the garden of the officers' mess. By then, the cuirassiers had stabled their horses and gathered under the venerable lime trees. There we would be received by the commanding officer, who would bid us welcome and call for a resounding three cheers for the honorary Commander-in-Chief – my mother. The day continued with a luncheon at the palace to which all the officers were invited with their wives, who were dressed in their finery. Incidentally, one of these ladies was the daughter of our dear 'Old Man' – Mr. Heath. She was married to ADC A. Mordvinov, whom we had known since our early childhood.

The evening was the best because then we were all invited for dinner in the officers' mess, and this was great fun. Sometimes we danced a little, sometimes there was a little 'divertissement' or some of us would go up to the billiard room – an open gallery over the big hall in which we had dined – to talk or just listen to the orchestra playing in the gallery opposite.

The Cuirassier Regiment's gala day was one of the landmarks in our lives, and it probably became more so after Misha joined the regiment, where he rose to the rank of squadron commander a few years later. He was a real father to his soldiers, and they loved him dearly. When one of them was taken ill, he would visit him every day in the regiment's hospital and would often take me along too. If Misha was so busy that he could not manage to go himself, he would send me instead to find out how the patient was getting on. I liked doing this – also because it gave me an opportunity to hear from them how much they loved Misha.

Every year we used to go for fishing expeditions for two days to a delightful place on a wide river with a watermill here and there, grassy banks and forest around in order to catch trout. We slept in a small wooden hut and got up before sunrise to go out on rafts, each with a man armed with a long pole that pushed the raft upstream. It was exciting to watch those big fish jump and rush around after our 'fly', which we manoeuvred along the surface. It sometimes took a while before we could land these strong big fellows so we first had to play with them and let them run away with a lot of our line, and then we slowly had to get them close enough to whisk them into the net. We became as sunburnt as niggers after the two days on that river. I caught my very first trout in the bubbling stream under the mill, and in my excitement and efforts to land my fish, I fell right into a bed of stinging nettles – face and hands! Once my mother, sister and brother-in-law accompanied us there with some friends for a day's fishing and we set off back to Gatchina in three motorcars. It was almost dark when we got close to the town and there we were suddenly met by the whole fire brigade. As the road was not very wide in that place, we all had to stop and then we found out that they had mistaken our strong lanterns for a fire. This was at the time when motorcars were very new.

These years were to be the happiest and most carefree in our lives. We enjoyed what there was to be enjoyed: small house parties, 'concours hippiques', Christmas parties in the regiment for each individual squadron, theatricals, races and much more. In summer we used to motor out with my mother and others in search of Misha, when he and the regiment were out at the manoeuvres. We often dined together in the officers' mess and spent lovely evenings with these friends, whose commander was the same General Derfelden, who had once helped me out of the crowd at Pskov in 1903.

At carnival time it was the custom to dress up and to drive with a group of one's friends from house to house – especially to those where one knew that there were other guests. One year Misha suggested that we put this old tradition into practice so we began to sew a lot of identical 'pierrot' costumes. We were a group of eleven conspirators: three ladies, four officers and four soldiers. When we put our masks on, we were so identical that it was impossible to tell one from the other and we ourselves could hardly find out who was who. In high spirits we drove off in open sledges to the house of an old captain, who was giving a ball that evening. We rang the bell, the door was opened, and without waiting for an invitation we all trooped in. Some of us were at once invited to dance, and we had great fun as no one could make out who we were. People tried to find out, be it just by our voices or by asking innumerable questions, but all the same no one succeeded. This amusing evening ended in the home of one of Misha's comrades where we sat round a tea table chatting and laughing at the evening's events.

Some years later Misha became commander of an army Hussar regiment, which was garrisoned in the town of Orel. So far, we had almost always been together so I missed him dreadfully – especially in the beginning. He seldom had time to come home on a visit, so I had to visit him and stayed for longer periods in the small, cosy house he had rented in that nice provincial town, where I felt most comfortable. To my delight I soon discovered how popular Misha was in his regiment, but I had, of course, not expected anything else. People could not but be fond of Misha. It was an excellent and most appealing regiment. Every week there was an evening when all the officers dined in the mess with their families and what fun we had. The band would play after dinner, and we would dance or just sit and talk.

I remember the second time I visited Misha. That was when some of the young officers from his regiment had arranged an amateur performance in the local theatre. It was quite a task they had embarked on. They had allied themselves with some talented young ladies and performed 'The Merry Widow' from beginning to end. It was really an exceptionally good amateur spectacle. The voices were lovely, and it was an enormous success and made the regiment even more popular than it already was. In the morning while Misha was occupied, I took long walks about the town, looked in at small shops or sat at home and chatted with his old servant – one of the dearest friends from our childhood, who loved a chat with me now and then and looked upon us as his own children and scolded us well when he thought it necessary – happily very rarely! Misha was kindness itself, soft-hearted and had a most loveable nature.

At the beginning of the war Misha was promoted to Division Commander for a division, which was solely made up of volunteers from the Caucasus. They were from all parts and all tribes and came bringing their horses, saddles and arms with them, each in his own characteristic attire. Among these horsemen were quite old men who considered it an honour to offer their lives and service in the Great War. WAR for them was something holy, and they were not afraid of death. In general, the Caucasians are a most chivalrous people – of a chivalry not of our generation and they are brave. They were mostly very good-looking, tall and thin and active like most mountain people. It was extremely difficult to deal with these horsemen, who had their own point of view on every subject. They had come of their own free will and disliked being ordered about. I remember one story which Misha told me and which is typical. One night the outposts were found calmly asleep. When awoken and told that this was quite wrong and in war time especially wrong, the men sullenly answered 'We are not at all afraid – if you are afraid, you may keep guard and keep awake too, but we need our sleep'. They could not be convinced as none of them had an idea about modern warfare. They only understood one thing: to attack, to rush down in a mad gallop and cut the enemy to pieces with their ancient sharp long swords, which had come down to them as heirlooms from their great-grandfathers. Nothing else meant anything to these men. If you only once saw such a division making an attack, you would not be surprised to hear that it was known as: 'The Savage Division'.

Yet they loved Misha and put all their faith in him and were always ready to give their lives for him. Even though Misha was happy to have so much devotion shown him, he must have had difficult times all the same since he had put up his tent at the foot of the Tower of Babel. His Caucasians came from all parts of the country and spoke so many different languages, so that it was only with the utmost difficulty that they could understand each other. Each one had his own personal view of how the war should be waged and since they had come of their own free will, they believed that they had the right to do as they thought best. This is why they more or less did what suited them. They hated to be ordered about. The majority of these proud, brave and wild warriors were staunch Mohammedans, which also caused some difficulties, especially if they fell ill or were wounded. I remember that we once had three men from 'The Savage Division' in our hospital. To start with, these poor people could not eat because the food had not been prepared by Mohammedans. We coaxed and begged, but the oldest of the three absolutely refused to eat until we offered him milk, eggs and fruit – this is what he allowed himself to partake of. Soon a special hospital was set up for these 'wild' people where surgeons, nurses and cooks were all Mohammedans, and then all went well.

All this and other worries wore Misha down, and when I met him in Kiev one day shortly before the outbreak of the revolution, he was both ill and tired. He was on his way home from the front to get a few days' rest in Gatchina and he certainly looked as if he needed it. He never got back to his 'Savage Division'. The great wave of the revolution, which swept over our heads, parted us for ever – in this world at least. He was such a dear and good brother and a wonderful person, who everyone was fond of.

CHAPTER 15

Who was Rasputin?

*T*he palaces and parks in Tsarskoe Selo were from about the same epoch as the Gatchina palace and park were and had all been built by prominent Italian architects, who Catherine II and her son Paul I had invited to Russia to show their art. Like Gatchina, Tsarskoe Selo was situated by a lake and the park was full of small pavilions – one more elegant in its architecture than the other. There were two palaces in Tsarskoe Selo. The big one was only used on formal occasions. The smaller one was my brother's residence and was where he always lived with his family. It stood in a park of its own, had a farm of its own and also a retirement home for old long-serving horses. There was even a horse cemetery where the names and dates of the horses buried there were engraved on special flagstones.

In the enormous so-called Catherine Park, there were numerous very beautiful and elegant pavilions. Small bridges spanned a brook or a canal here and there, a temple with columns disclosed an old Greek statue of Apollo or Venus half-hidden among lilac bushes, a marble bench stood invitingly in the shade of a stately oak and nearby a waterfall would spread coolness over its surroundings and make music for the ear. There was a special atmosphere over the Tsarskoe Selo park, and you would not have been surprised if, at the bend of the path, you would have seen the great Catherine herself as she walked along with her little dogs as she so often must have done in the years gone by. Tsarskoe Selo was full of the glory of bygone days and evoked a feeling of melancholy. In the middle of the lake there stood a tall bronze pillar on a stone foundation. One day I visited this place in a boat and saw on that occasion that there was a door at the bottom of some steps, which apparently led to a secret passage. The door was locked, as no one was allowed down there because it was dangerous. It was said that the passage led under the whole lake and out into one of the many fantastic buildings in the park. How I longed to explore that long tunnel under the lake, but I never had an opportunity to do so.

The park round the royal residence was two hundred years younger than the Catherine Park. In it were also many strange buildings – mainly from the time of the Romantic Movement. One of these small buildings was called 'the Ruin' – it looked like a church that had been shot to pieces. It only had one room and in it *stood a large figure of Christ. Another building was of a more recent date – a sort of chalet that stood on the banks of a lake. It had its own sad story. My father's grandfather, the Emperor Nicholas I, had several children and among them a young and very beautiful daughter, Alexandra. She was married to a brother of my maternal Danish grandmother Queen Louise. The Grand Duchess Alexandra was, however, fairly delicate, and when she felt unwell, she would make a habit of spending some time in the little chalet.*

It is said that the young couple was supposed to have moved to Denmark and lived at Bernstorff, but the Grand Duchess's weak constitution prevented them from travelling. A year later she gave birth – but she was much too weak to pull through the strain of the birth, and both mother and daughter lost their lives. In memory of his beloved daughter, the Emperor arranged for a sculptor to carve a huge marble angel holding a tiny child in its arms which was then placed outside the little chalet. The angel had Alexandra's features and hairstyle and looked so lovingly at the little child, which had cost her her life. It was such a beautiful monument and made such a deep impression on me.

There is much poetry and romance about Tsarskoe Selo. A lot has disappeared and will never come back again. *By now, the park has probably been opened to the public. I often think of the people who go there and wonder whether they can hear the past whisper in the leaves of the gnarled oak trees, and are able to listen to the tongues of springs and fountains telling tales of bygone times. Perhaps they are deaf to the voices of the past and don't think about it, but just sit around and pass the time on Catherine's old marble benches, throw stones at the fish or frogs from the delicate bridges or scribble their names on the walls of the temples and bowers. The thought makes me quite melancholic – Tsarskoe Selo was such a part of Russia's history.*

It was in these surroundings that my nieces lived and grew up. They looked forward to going to Peterhof every summer and especially much to going on trips on the 'Standart', the yacht, which took them to the Finnish archipelago for a cruise of two to three weeks. They travelled with their parents and I was

Emperor Nicholas II with Tsarevich Alexis on the beach, ca. 1912.

always invited to join them. My nieces loved these trips and enjoyed every single minute on board and I loved being with them! It was so beautiful among all those tiny islands, which were so overgrown with pine trees. Here and there you would catch a glimpse of a small, red-painted farmhouse or a cow, which was slowly munching away at the lush green grass in a little meadow. It was so peaceful everywhere, but just slightly 'oppressive' – like it is in the north of Sweden. When the ship moored at one of the islands, we would go for long walks with the officers from the yacht, or arrange small excursions taking packed lunches with us. It also happened that we arranged picnics for the sailors and invited young Finnish girls to dance with them. We would sit nearby and enjoy watching the dancing. The sailors, who had also served on the 'Polar Star', and who had been in Copenhagen, knew the modern dances from Tivoli or perhaps it was from the basement bars in the sailor's district of Nyhavn. These sailors knew what it was all about and were the 'beaus' of the ball.

The best of all evenings was the Midsummer Eve's festival. Then we would all go ashore on one of the little islands, light a huge bonfire and chat and sing through the whole light, warm summer night. *On that occasion the sailors would play a funny game. They would bend young fir trees down to the ground, catch hold of their tops and swing themselves up high and then down again – again and again. It looked most amusing. When the 'Standart' did not anchor for the night, but continued the voyage, we would spend the evenings on deck. My brother would play a game of dominoes with the officers, and we would sit around on deck with our needlework and chat with the others. We enjoyed the air and the view. Every evening at 7½ there were prayers on deck for everyone – the sky was yellow or orange with pink evening clouds – it was so quiet. I often think of those evenings of peace and beauty among the Finnish islands – the quiet calm water and the dark outlines of the pinewoods and rocks against the evening sky. Little did we know of what was to come and the trials we were to endure.*

I am often questioned about a man, whose name has been in many mouths – so often that it is very difficult to say anything that people have not already heard and which are mostly lies. So much has been put down to him, his power and influence that his name has become known far and wide – and yet – Gregory Rasputin was a simple peasant from Siberia, who could hardly sign his own name. He was born with a magnetic power, which can be more or less pronounced in any-one anywhere in the world. Such people belong to the category of 'wise men' or 'wise women'. Of course, the closer you get to the Orient, where there is less so-called culture, the easier it is for such people to develop their powers. Rasputin had these magnetic powers, and as he lived in a place, where the so-called culture did not

The Tsarevich, Grand Duke Alexis Nicholaievich being carried ashore, 1913.
He is wearing the cap from the Imperial Yacht Штандарт (Standart).

put a stop to him in any way and where people blindly believed in his mystical powers, he was able to develop them to such a degree, which hardly would have been possible under more civilized conditions.

The rumour of Gregory Rasputin's magnetic abilities spread far and wide – and finally reached the Imperial court. Shortly after, the accident happened when my nephew Alexei, the young heir to the throne, who had been born with that dreadful bleeding illness, tripped when he jumped into a boat from the bank. He had no visible injuries but the fall had caused an internal bleeding, which could not be stopped. Even though the best doctors were summoned, there was no one who could help him and the little boy suffered dreadful pains. The situation took such a dangerous turn that Alexei was almost dying, and my brother and sister-in-law were naturally beside themselves with concern. Then someone suggested that they

Gregory Efimovich Rasputin with Colonel Lomar and
Major-General Prince Putyatin, 1914.

telegraph to Rasputin in Siberia. He answered immediately: 'The child will get well', and from that moment the temperature started to drop and the pains lessened. It didn't take long before Alexei was on his feet again. Anyone, who has someone they are fond of, will understand that Alexei's parents were full of gratitude after this incident and that they felt reassured whenever Rasputin was nearby. One could never know when Alexei would have another attack.

Even though I often visited my brother and his family, I have only met Rasputin twice. He resembled quite an 'ordinary' simple peasant. The only thing about him that made any 'special' impression on me – were his eyes. They were huge and pale blue under long eye lashes and thick brows. When he looked at you, he had the habit of first narrowing his eyes and then suddenly opening them which gave you the feeling that they grew bigger and bigger. Then he would stare at you with wide open eyes which gave you the feeling that they could pierce right through you and discover your innermost secrets. He really had strange eyes. I have also spoken with him. He talked to me about my life and asked if he could come to see me – I said that he could, but he never came. He used a lot of scripture words and phrases in his conversation, but that was not strange at the time since so many of our peasants, who very often could neither read nor write, knew the New Testament by heart.

Now, as I look back, I can clearly draw a parallel between much of what preceded the French revolution and what happened in Russia. In both countries, the elements, who wanted to start a revolution, first had to find a method to undermine the people's natural love and veneration of their sovereigns. Therefore people had to be found, who could be used to do this work. In Russia the bad elements also turned their attention to Rasputin, who walked in and out of the Emperor's palace. Rasputin himself was too simple-minded to fathom the depth of what was going on around him and how his name was being used. He was probably amused and pleased that people in the capital made so much fuss of him and invited him into their homes where they treated him to good food and noble wines. At the same time they naturally flattered him which appealed to his vanity. That is human nature. In the end he became a passive tool in their hands and was one of the aces, which the revolutionaries played out in their fight against the empire. There is, however, no doubt that he – perhaps without knowing it himself – did his bit to put the snowball into motion, and when the first one started to roll, it grew bigger and bigger without anyone being able to stop it until finally – like an avalanche – it pulled both the guilty and the innocent down into the abyss.

CHAPTER 16

The Emperor and the Runaway

My mother spent the first summer months of 1914 in England with her sister, Queen Alexandra.

The two sisters were very fond of each other and enjoyed their time together. They started to make plans for a continuation of their holiday at their beloved 'Hvidøre', and the day for their departure was set for the end of July. Then, however, rumours about a coming war made my mother change her mind. Even though she did not for a moment believe that there was danger afoot for Russia, and that it would be wound up in such a conflict, she set off home to Russia. Mother travelled through Germany, but got no further than Berlin, where the war caught up with her. She was told that war had broken out and her train would not go further. She was obliged to turn back and go to Denmark, where she could pay the family a short visit before continuing on through Sweden to Finland, and finally getting back safely to St. Petersburg. Mother's journey went smoothly and we were naturally happy to have her home again safe and sound. We could, however, only spend a very short time in each other's company because I left for the front with a hospital train three days after Mother's arrival. We left St. Petersburg on one of the first days in August. We were 18 nurses, 5 doctors and had everything with us for 200 beds.

At the last minute before the train started, our head doctor was given a written order telling us where we would be going. Our destination was a small town called Rovno. Then the departure signal was given and off we went. Our train drove very slowly and sometimes we had the feeling that it was crawling along the lines. It would stop incredibly many times to let other trains with soldiers pass on their way to the front. They would hang out of the windows as they drove past, sing at the tops of their voices and wave to us. We waved back even though they did not give the impression of being unhappy, but no doubt they were in a little need of some modest encouragement. This time it was neither the case of a parade or manoeuvres but a conflict where lives were at stake.

The journey went on and on, day after day and lasted for three days. We only had hot food once a day. Then the train would stop at a station and we would all get off and have a meal in one big amiable group. On those occasions we were always in high spirits and the head doctor was the happiest and jolliest of us all.

*Grand Duchess Olga Alexandrovna in her nurse's uniform reading
by a window, 1914.*

Otherwise, the doctors kept apart, and we only saw them from the windows or when we were eating. An exception was the head doctor, who from time to time would burst into our compartment to tell us how fond he was of nurses and that he wouldn't know what to do without them. He would make us all laugh so much with his funny stories so that the noise must even have been heard by the engine driver. Then he would dash off again just as quickly as he had arrived. His short visits cheered us up, and all eighteen of us would have been more than happy to go through fire and water for his sake. Otherwise, the hours in the train were passed drinking tea. We each had a tin mug, and hot water was to be had anywhere. It was a cosy time chatting and getting to know each other.

On August 14th we reached Kiev, where we were told upon arrival that there would be a stop for several hours. We were very pleased since we were all most eager to see this historic and pretty town in great detail. Our excitement reached boiling point when the head doctor suggested that we all go together to visit the old monastery, which lay high above the River Dnieper. We went up there by tram. It climbed up and up in an eternity and finally stopped not far from the white walls of the monastery. After having seen the inside of the huge cathedral we proceeded down endless steps to the catacombs. We were told that these narrow passages, cut out in the moist sandstone, were kilometres long and stretched far down under the Dnieper. It was a strange feeling. At certain points the passages widened and there we noticed small chapels. Of course, we were all equipped with wax candles and had a monk to guide us. He made a point of telling us to keep close together, but I am sure that we would have found that out ourselves, as it didn't last long before we discovered how awful it would be to lose one's way down there in the damp darkness in that maze of passages. I do not know how the others experienced it, but I came up to the daylight with a feeling of human insignificance and mediocrity. But at the same time, the town was a witness to the power and influence of Christianity on human souls. It had been in Kiev that St. Vladimir had first preached the gospels of Christ in the year 987.

After eight days and nights of continued travel in our train we at last arrived at our destination – Rovno. Most of the inhabitants there were Jews. The town had but one street with shops. All the small streets were very narrow and dirty and swarmed with filthy children of all ages. Our field hospital was housed in some empty barracks, which had previously been used as quarters for an artillery regiment. The soldiers had departed for the front leaving several cats and dogs forlorn and sad behind. They would nip in and out through doors and windows in search of a little food just hoping that their friends, the soldiers, would come back and give them something to eat like they used to. Of course, we could not resist their imploring eyes, so took care of them with the result that they stayed with us during the war no matter where we were.

The first thing we had to do at our new location was to stuff the 200 mattresses with hay and sew them up. Then we had to air the blankets in the sun, inspect the wards and make everything ready to receive the wounded.

It was a very busy time. All was in order when one hot afternoon three days later our first patients arrived. I will never forget that afternoon. Suddenly, we heard the distant scraping of wheels on the hard road. The sound grew louder and louder, and then we could see where it came from. One cart after the other was making its way towards us – it looked like a whole train of carts and each one was full of wounded soldiers. The carts drove up to our doors and the transfer of the wounded started. It was a dreadful start to our work. The terrible sound of creaking wheels and ringing hooves haunted me for days when trying to sleep. Again and again, I would jump out of bed and rush to the windows to see if it was true that more casualties were arriving or whether it was just my tired brain that was imagining that dreadful sound, which meant so much suffering for so many happy young men. They were all admiringly brave. These poor suffering soldiers never complained and were grateful for anything one did for them. They were in a dreadful state when they arrived – dusty and blood-stained. Their clothes were often quite stiff with dry blood, and we had to cut them to pieces as one could not take them off otherwise. Our two hundred beds were not enough – the casualties kept on arriving. We then had to put the lightly wounded soldiers on mattresses in the entrance halls and corridors. The first days we worked without stopping, not knowing whether it was day or night, without rest and only eating what we were able to grab on the run. It was a pressure that I later could not understand that we could cope with. There was simply not a single moment for a break. Then the worst rush was over and some sort of order was brought into our lives; it was really only then that we started taking pleasure in our work. How one gets to love one's patients and what a joy it is to see them recover, or how rewarded one feels when they show their gratitude and affection. Many were the letters I had to 'write home' for my patients, but I was never allowed to write that they were wounded, not to frighten 'the old folks' at home!"

One day we were informed that my eldest brother was on his way home from inspecting the troops in the Caucasus and that he would be stopping in Rovno to visit our wounded. That created quite a stir. The doctors only thought about clean sheets and blankets, gave orders for the floors to be washed again and again and that the windows should be cleaned so that the Emperor could see that it was a proper hospital. I am quite sure that he soon discovered that it was because

Watercolours by Grand Duchess Olga Alexandrovna: Young soldier in sick bed reading, November 8th, 1914. Nicholas Kulikovsky, Grand Duchess Olga Alexandrovna's future husband, November 15th, 1914.

he could clearly see it – not by looking at the sheets or the windows – but when he looked at the wounded. When the patients heard that the Emperor would be visiting them, even the weariest and weakest of them beamed with happiness. They so looked forward to seeing the person for whom they had shed their blood and risked life and limb. *And then he arrived. Wandering from ward to ward my brother spoke kindly to each single patient and we saw how their faces lit up at his approach, and followed him till he disappeared into the next ward. Only one of the wounded soldiers was very sad and bitter. He had his eyes bandaged up because they were so weak that the doctors did not want to take the risk of exposing them to daylight. Just before his turn came to be spoken to, he mumbled 'to think that my only chance to see my Emperor is being wasted'. I heard this and ran to ask the head doctor to ask if his bandages might be taken off for a minute while the Emperor was there – and his wish was fulfilled. The soldier stared at my brother with an expression, which said that his dearest wish had come true.*

On the other side of the road, there was a military hospital. I knew the head doctor there quite well. We were great friends because I helped him to get many things his military hospital was short of. Our Red Cross hospitals were ever so much richer than the military ones. While we were doing the rounds of the wards over there, this nice doctor took me by the arm and said: 'You must help me. We have got a young soldier here – a runaway. He is dreadfully wounded and when he is more or less well again, he will be shot. Please intercede with your brother'. I promised, and soon had an opportunity to whisper my prayer into my brother's ear. Soon after, we stood at the bed of the runaway, which was easy to find as a sentinel stood next to it. Before my brother or anyone could prevent him, the miserable and badly wounded boy crept out of his bed and fell at his Emperor's feet. He was so pale-faced and so young – a mere boy. My brother put his hand on his shoulder and said: 'You are forgiven' and turning to the sentinel, he said: 'you can go!' We helped the wounded soldier back into bed, and my brother asked him why he had run away. The answer came among sobs: 'I … was so … afraid, I ran away … into a forest … they shot at me and caught me.' I looked round and saw that the doctors and nurses all stood there with lowered heads and with tears in their eyes. My brother looked at the poor boy. His eyes were moist. A single tear ran down his weather-beaten cheek and settled in his beard.

Countess Zinaide Mengden*: The Departure of the Empress Marie Feodorovna from England – 1914.

The day of our departure was finally decided on and we received telegrams from the countries we would be passing through on the way home. The Empress's private train waited in Calais and needed "laissez passers" to get through ... We sailed in a steamship from Dover to Calais and there we got into our own Russian train and travelled through France. Grand Duchess Xenia and her lady-in-waiting joined us at the Belgian border and continued the journey with us.

When we crossed the German border we still did not know that the war had already broken out. But from the mood of the German people at the station, from the insults that they showered us with, we sensed their hostility, so we had a notion of what had happened. In Berlin we met our Russian ambassador Sverbeyev and two German gentlemen, who had been sent by the Emperor Wilhelm to inform the Empress that war had been declared and that it was impossible to reach Russian as planned since the bridge at the frontier had been blown up. She was given the choice between going to Switzerland or Denmark. She naturally chose the latter. Here in Berlin Grand Duchess Xenia's daughter Irene and her husband Prince Youssupov and his parents got into our train. We then had to travel back to Kiel and continued on from there to Denmark ... We stayed in Copenhagen for some days: the Empress went to Hvidøre and the rest of us were put up at the Hotel d'Angleterre. It was swarming with Russians who had fled from Germany in great haste and who were nearly all without luggage and money.

Source: "The Memoirs of the Countess Zinaide Mengden"*, page 86

Diary Tatiana Nicholaievna: Grand Duchess Olga Alexandrovna's Departure for the War.

Friday, 1st August 1914

I had a lesson. At 11 o'clock we drove to Grandmother's. From there we took A. Olga home to us. She spent a little while with Mama and us. Then we said good-bye to her and she left. [She was friendly with the Grand Duchesses and corresponded with them].

In the afternoon she left with the parish hospital Saint Eugenie [The general Red Cross hospital Saint Eugenie was founded in 1893 and was given its name in honour of the Imperial patroness – the Princess Eugenie Maximilianovna of Oldenburg. It was situated in St. Petersburg on the Old Russian Street 3. Today the municipal hospital No. 46 is located in the building]. *She is going to the war as a sister of mercy.*

We five had breakfast with Papa and Mama. In the afternoon we went for a walk like we did yesterday, had a go on the swings and got caught in the rain. We had tea with Papa and Mama and chatted on the telephone with N.P. and N.N. I sent my photograph to N.P. yesterday. We had dinner with Papa and Mama at Grandmother's. A. Xenia and U. Sandro were there too.

Afterwards, Kostia [Konstantine Konstantinovich, Prince, aide-de-camp, staff-captain of the Ismailovsky Life-Guards Regiment, son of Grand Duke Konstantin Konstantinovich] *came to say good-bye. He is leaving tomorrow with the Ismailovsky Regiment to go to the war. We went home at ten thirty. Papa read.*

Source: GARF (Russian State Archives, Moscow)

Olga Alexandrovna to her niece Tatiana Nicholaievna

2nd August 1914 in the train on the way to war.

My dear sweet darling Tatiana

*I felt very touched by your dear letter yesterday evening!
We should have left at 9½ but stood still at the station till 12½.
There was a crowd there – friends of the sisters and their relatives –
and when we finally started moving, they all made the sign of the
cross over us through the open windows. I did not sleep particularly
well since the bugs tormented us all! – How loathsome – Horrible!*

Tatiana Andreevna [Gromova] *is very sweet and cheerful.
Just next to me is a very likeable and unassuming nun – together
we hunted bugs this morning and she cleaned my sofa with her hair
brush. She is such a dear, but it embarrassed me terribly! We are
travelling in a second class carriage – there is a corridor down the
middle – compartments on one side and arm chairs on the other,
which are used as beds in the night. We washed in turns. Everyone
is terribly kind to me. The Princess* [Eugenie Maximilianovna of
Oldenburg, Duchess of Leuchtenberg – GD Olga's first mother-in-law –
1845–1925] *was at the station and said that she wished she could
turn into a fly so that she could flutter into my carriage! I can
imagine how she would buzz around and disturb our sleep...*

There has just been a stop – at Dno Station [it was here during
the night of 2nd March 1917 that Nicholas II signed a deed of abdication
for his son and himself, in favour of his brother Michael. This took place
in the Imperial train, which could not reach Petrograd and was stood in
a siding at the station of Dno, near Pskov in the province of Vitebsk].
*We drank milk and had a meal of sausage and bread. The doctors
came into our compartment to chat. We are on the way to Kiev, and
from there we do not know where they will send us. We are travelling
through places where the after-effects of local fires are visible.*

*I think so much about you – my darlings, my loved ones! Tell
Mama* [the Empress Alexandra Feodorovna] *that I am so touched that
I cannot say in words how much she means to me and that I love her
ever so much.*

It is raining slightly, which is good so that there is no dust. But the bugs?! It is disgusting to think about them; the sister says that it will get worse and that we will get lice in our hair.

I kiss dear Olga and Marie and Nastenka "a gloomy one". I embrace dear Papa and Grandmother [the Empress Marie Feodorovna] and Aunt Xenia. Tell Grandmother that she should not be offended that I wrote to you first but that was an answer to your letter. I visited Irina. She is terribly sweet and thin, talks a lot and is happy. Goodbye, my own darling!

May the Lord take care of you! Write to me frequently, my dears.

I love you with all my heart. Aunt Olga

Source: GARF (Russian State Archives, Moscow)

Olga to her niece Tatiana Nicholaievna.

25th September 1914

My sweet darling, Tatiana, dear!

I think a lot about you – are you having news from friends? A big thank-you to you for your last letter. I did not manage to send off a letter to you with U. Sandro's courier, but I will write and send it with the next one. I have received a lengthy and wonderfully nice letter from the "colonel". I try to write to him as often as possible. He sent me six letters by mail and all six of them did not get here. As a rule, letters do not reach us. Our nurses and doctors don't receive any either, but when they get them, it is clear that people have been writing them letters every day. Many of our patients have left, and at first I missed them – because they were mine; but now I have become fond of (and loved) three dears – two without legs and a third seriously wounded in the thigh and injured in the blood-vessels, which is really dangerous – God give that he will get well again. One without a leg was in the Combined Guards' Battalion in 1905–1907 and was incredibly pleased to see me and to remember with me all the places like Gatchina, T[sarskoe] S[elo], Christmas – etc. He is so affectionate and now one of his dreams is to go to Petrograd to see Papa "my father", as he calls him and he said that with such a radiant smile! I will send him there for a leg and when he is there – please visit him – I will write where he will be staying!

The third one – with wonderfully black eyes – was badly burnt, and now his eye lashes, eye brows and moustache are still hardly visible! He is very fond of me, waves his hand to me and shouts: "My dear darling sister, come over to me and sit down with me". He says that he loves me like "his own mother". He is so sweet!

Today, I gave six cigarettes from Papa to each of them and explained who they were from. They were so happy and grateful for this dear gesture. Some decided to keep theirs as a souvenir, so I had to explain to them that they had been sent to be smoked, but one they could keep as a souvenir. And my black-eyed friend – Sladkevitch, says: "give me some more, I am passionately fond of smoking", and I answered him that I would write to Papa and say that here is such a glutton and extravagant man called Sladkevitch – who for no reason whatsoever has smoked all the good cigarettes!

He laughed a lot and was pleased about this! I am also very much afraid for him because suddenly today pus seeped out the stump – that is not at all good and he himself was frightened and sobbed terribly this morning, poor darling! I just sat on his bed and fed semolina to another one who was sitting, actually lying, next to him. Well, the Colonel writes that young Bely will be married to Anna Ioanovna Sokolova's daughter! Would you have wanted to marry Bely? No, that is what I thought. Imagine him in civilian clothes!!! When I think about someone, who I like – I picture them in civilian clothes – and then only those – who I really love – will stand up to my criticism! The poor little wife of a pilot has arrived from Sevastopol and is now staying with us for a while, and then she will meddle in a hospital train. She knows absolutely nothing – but runs after Tatiana Andreevna and is dressed like a nurse.

Here almost everyone is dressed as imaginary nurses – and all those fools parading along the streets really make me angry. It will always be the same – that happened in the last war – when women – who wanted to amuse themselves, dressed up as nurses. At one time, even school girls walked around here in short skirts and fluttering kerchiefs and with the Red Cross on their sleeves!

I do not know if Papa receives (probably not) the army bulletin published by the staff of General Ivanov – it is a very good little newspaper – and yesterday I found one article in it which made me cry alone in my room – it was the letter from a mother to a son – an officer in the war.

I will copy it for you: "Your father was killed not far from us at Liayan; I have sent you off on a holy cause, for the protection of our dear homeland from the close and terrible enemy. Remember that you are the son of a hero! My heart aches and my eyes weep when I say to you "Be worthy of him!" I well know the dreadful fateful horror of these words and in spite of them and the torment for you, I repeat them. We will all die, what is our life? It is just a drop in the ocean of beautiful Russia. We will all die, but let our country flourish and rejoice. I know that we will be forgotten, our *happy descendants will not remember those, who rot away in common graves. I am kissing and blessing you – I am saying farewell to you. When they send you off to the fighting, do not remember my tears, remember only my blessings ....May God keep you, my darling, my joy, my love ... something else:* THE ENEMIES, *they write this everywhere,* ARE EVIL AND WILD, BUT DO NOT GIVE WAY TO BLIND VENGEANCE, DO NOT RAISE YOUR HAND TO ANYONE STRUCK DOWN AND BE GRACIOUS TO THOSE WHO FATE PUTS IN YOUR HAND"...

This letter was found on the tortured son. "In wild and vindictive madness – says the writer, – the frenzied German barbarians and killers had found time to torture the hero before finishing him off. The letter was splattered with blood – a relic to be kept in sacred memory of this family".

What wild horror... There is another similar story, but I will write it to someone else as it is now time to finish this letter. Tatiana Andreevna is also sitting nearby on the same window sill and is also writing to one of you. They have stopped giving me elixir to drink! The cough has stopped. The cold is intense and it is stormy (force 10). I send many greetings to Nic. Pav. and Mordvinov, he should write – letters should be sent through my office, otherwise they do not arrive.

It is with the greatest affection that I embrace the entire darling family starting with Papa and ending with Alexei! God bless you, my darling!

Always your Aunt Olga

It has been said that Papa will visit us tomorrow morning! The soldiers are radiant! I am too. God bless you! We are going to Yaroslav in three days.

Source: GARF (Russian State Archives, Moscow)

Olga Alexandrovna to her niece Maria Nicholaievna

Rovno, 5–6th October 1914

Hello my dear little fatty one, my darling Maria!

Was it interesting at the parade of the convoy? I deeply regret that I never see it – especially this one would have interested me very much. As soon as I got up, a telegram was delivered to me from them, in which they congratulate me themselves and write very dear things. I feel dreadfully sorry for Oleg and his family and especially for Nadia Petrovna, who loved him dearly. But young Oleg had a glorious death! We have had a lot of work in recent days as there were about two hundred new casualties here.

Among them were many different Cossacks: Terskies, Kubans and Don Cossacks. They are such dears. Some of them were dreadfully wounded. We have one very dear cornet here. Today, I invited him for a walk in the garden and that made him very happy. The nurses took a picture of us and I made a photographic pose with my legs (drawing) – do you understand? It pleased him so much that he immediately did the same! There was one terribly dear and very young wounded volunteer Cossack, who I took care of myself as I did not entrust him to anyone else and did not permit anyone to touch him and growled and clenched my teeth when any of the nurses decided to help me to dress him! For him that was very nice and flattering so he laughed a lot – and his comrades did that too – and when we left, we gave each other a firm handshake and he said "I will never forget you!" Then I also have an old Tatar whom I am very fond of – he resembles a monkey – and he is so pitiful and suffers. He is injured from the thigh to the arm. Today, he was operated on so that the pus could be removed from the wounds – the poor thing was under chloroform. Several Georgians are also here, but they are not really interesting. My Orenburg Suvorov writes – he was taken to hospital in Kursk but wanted to go to Kharkov – since that is where his regiment is stationed in peacetime!

I really am so fond of Tatiana Andreevna, and we live very comfortably together. Vera Titova took the pen, which Papa signed his name with when he was here with us – and her friend Vera Pommerg took the chair on which his a... [arse] had been and sat on it for two minutes – and then she tied a pink bow on the back of it and is jealously protecting it from anyone who wants to touch it! Today, I stood for a long time and watched how the warriors were training close to our barracks. They were learning well.

The medical orderlies are housed right under my room and are at the present moment singing evening prayers and ended with a hymn. Every word is audible ....the first time, the hymn was not successful and stopped in the middle and they argued and then started again... I have just received your letter and all the other ones too – this is a real lie – since I received them early this morning, but there was no time to read them as about 150 casualties were brought here and we spent five hours non-stop bandaging them up! I then begged for mercy! We had dinner late and I went out to have some fresh air. From my Kukushkin [Kulikovsky Nicholas Alexandrovich] I have today received a proper dispatch! I was very happy – as I hadn't heard from him for a long time – and felt really worried. Well goodbye my dear, a big thank you to Olga and Nastyushka for the letters and greetings from the nurses; I am thankful to you all and greet you. T.A. kisses you all; she is busy and could not write.

Loving you, Aunt Olga

Source: GARF (Russian State Archives, Moscow)

CHAPTER 17

My Own Regiment

I *was only 19 when I was married. On the day I left my rooms at Gatchina on my eldest brother's arm to walk over to the church, we were met by a deputation from a regiment in an unusual brown uniform unlike any other. It was the only regiment in the whole army which was entitled to wear this special uniform. The deputation stood to attention as we approached. We stopped in front of them, and my brother presented me: 'Here is your new honorary Commander-in-Chief'.*

I do not think that I resembled an 'honorary' commander as I was dressed in gala with two long curls dangling down on either shoulder, but all the same I was ever so delighted at such an honour and such a present. I already knew the regiment well, which had now been assigned to me, and that it was one of the most famous in Russia.

Suddenly I was reminded of a day when as a young girl I was sitting at the window in my father's study after lunch and looking out into the street. He was sitting at his desk smoking a cigarette. A soldier in a strange uniform was passing and I called out: 'Papa, come here quick – look, what sort of a solider is it in that brown uniform?' Father got up quickly, came over to the window and said: 'That is an Akhtyrsky soldier. He belongs to a very good old regiment.' And then Father told me that the brown uniform dated from the time of the war with Napoleon. The Akhtyrsky Regiment had distinguished itself on a number of battlefields. They had also been in the line of fire in 1814 with the result that their uniforms were tattered and torn. When the war was over, this brave regiment was to take part in the big parade in Paris, but could not turn up in their ragged uniforms. They were now in dire straits, so a kindly officer thought of ordering material for new uniforms from a Benedictine monastery, where the monks' cowls were brown. In memory of this, and as a thank-you for their good service during the whole war, the soldiers have been equipped with brown uniforms ever since. Well – so now I was an honorary Commander-in-Chief! It brought the memory of my dear father closer. I was touched, happy and proud all at the same time, and I have never had a reason to regret that I accepted that honorary appointment. I think I can say that the regiment and I became real friends on that very first day and have been friends ever since!

My regiment was stationed at Medzibosh, which was not far from the

Austrian border. All the same, I kept in contact with it and its officers as well as I could. Whenever one of 'my' officers came to St. Petersburg, he would invariably come to see me and I knew them all. And when a young officer was transferred to the Akhtyrsky Regiment, he would always visit his honorary colonel before leaving for Medzibosh.

In the year 1902 I went abroad and on the way home from it I had an opportunity to visit the regiment in Medzibosh. It was late in the autumn and snow had already started to fall. I was met at the small station by the commander of the regiment, Colonel Benois, who drove me to their head-quarters 20 kilometres away. He was a kind, fatherly man and understood that I was somewhat uneasy about the situation, so explained to me in his obliging manner how I was expected to 'perform' upon my arrival. He also went through the program, which the regiment had prepared for the two days I was going to spend at headquarters. Even though the colonel was most understanding, there were nevertheless moments during that long drive when I regretted my decision and longed to be home again and hide under my bed ... but there I was – and it was too late to regret. I had to stick it out to the bitter end! Fortunately, the experience did not turn out to be in the least bit bitter. When I finally got there, I felt most comfortable and enjoyed life to the full.

Medzibosh is a white, medieval fortress, which had once belonged to the Turks. Its walls were several metres thick and it stood most picturesquely high up on a spot where the river Bug makes a bend. The only road up to the fortress leads along a steep slope, which was so slippery on the day we arrived that it was almost impossible to negotiate the cobblestones. We did, however, manage, and made our entry into one of the inner courtyards through the low gateway in the metre-thick wall. There we were welcomed by the regiment, which was lined up for a parade. The brown-clad soldiers stood there unwaveringly like pillars of stone, and while the band played the regimental march, the colonel and I walked along the line – followed by many pairs of friendly yet curious eyes. My heart hammered so excitedly in step with the music that it was almost painful, and yet, it was a joy to see them all. I was about to both laugh and cry at the same time, because I was so happy to meet my comrades and friends again.

When the parade was over, I went with the colonel over to his lodgings where I made the acquaintance of his wife and their three young daughters. The rooms were very dark and the windows mere slits in the wall – better suited for firing a gun through than to let in the daylight. That evening we all dined in the officers' mess. Most of the men were single – in all there were only about seven married men in the whole garrison. That evening made an unforgettable impression on me, partly because it was so cosy and partly because one of the soldiers serving at table spilt the contents of a gravy boat over my shoulder and down my new white dress. I must have looked quite a pretty sight for the rest of that evening! The incident did not affect my good spirits, more to put a good word in for the unlucky soldier. I had noticed his horrified face when the accident happened and heard the colonel hiss 'you idiot' between his teeth as he walked past.

Among the officers in this regiment were three brothers by the name of Panaev. They were loved by all at headquarters. The eldest of them, Boris, was typically ascetic. He never drank wine and slept on the floor with his saddle under his head for a pillow – he was just like an ancient crusader. Boris was a plucky soldier and so good and noble that he was shown more respect than his years of service entitled him to have. His word was law and his soldiers went through fire and water for his sake. Boris especially looked after his younger comrades and infected them with his shining example. His two younger brothers were extremely first rate fellows too. Guri was my age and the youngest, Lev a year younger.

After the dinner and during the pleasant evening some of the younger officers started telling me ghost stories. They said that the old castle was haunted and that if I heard clinking spurs and clanking chains, I could be sure that this was the ghost. I have never believed in ghosts, but all the same I was somewhat frightened when I went to bed in my turret room around midnight. Happily, the ghost had a night off, so did not come and visit me, and once I had fallen asleep, I slept peacefully and well.

The next morning there was another parade. I rigged myself out in my Akhtyrsky uniform which made quite an impression. Guri Panaev fetched me and helped me onto a horse called Petunia, and then the two of us rode down the steep, icy cobblestone hill till we got to the field where the whole regiment was lined up on their horses. For the rest of that day I was taken about to see how the different squadrons were billeted in the area. They lived with the peasants in their cottages and were spread over a very big area. Each squadron had its own smithy, kitchen etc. Two days later the hour of parting came and I was just as unhappy when I had to leave as I was when I had to go there two days previously.

Fifteen years passed before I again had an opportunity to visit my regiment. 13 years added to 1902 makes 1915 – and that meant that the regiment had gone to war. For a while it had been stationed on the foremost line, but it had been pulled back to a village for a rest and I had been asked to come and visit them for a couple of days. At that time I was living in Kiev, and there I happened to meet about six or seven officers, who were on leave. When it was time for them to return to their regiment, I travelled back with them. We had a railway carriage all to ourselves and had a jolly time. One of the officers was a real virtuoso on the harmonica and never grew tired of playing – nor we of listening. A dreadful snow storm was howling when we arrived in the Austrian village of Zavadovka, and when we found the regiment, it was almost snowed up. It didn't stop snowing for the next two days with the result that the snow drifted up against the doors and windows, so that we were completely snowed in for four days. I shared a peasant's hut with four officers. It had two rooms, a big one, where four officers slept and a small one behind it, which was mine! On the first evening two of my neighbours began a discussion, which started quietly, but gradually their voices grew louder and louder so that I could not possibly get to sleep. It was finally too much for me, so I opened the door a little and threw one of my snow-boots at the loudest man. That helped, and from then on there was dead silence. The next morning they begged my pardon and all five of us had a good laugh. The officer, who had been the victim, said that none of the bombs he had experienced had made such an impression on him as my missile. One of them drew a caricature of us all – including the snow-boot!

During the time I visited the regiment, we twice had an important guest in our humble quarters. It was General Mannerheim, who had been invited to dine with us. There wasn't much room but 'where there is room in the heart, there is room in the house'. We sat down to table on stools, boxes and beds with candles burning in bottles and sang songs and chatted until the candles had burnt down. That was the signal to say goodnight.

As soon as the weather improved, we would go out in sledges or those men, who still had good horses, would arrange a 'concour hippique' in the deep snow while the rest of us would sit in the snow wrapped up in warm coats and watch. On the day I left, the whole regiment accompanied me on my way on horseback. The soldiers rode quite slowly next to my sledge and sang all my favourite songs. To this day, I can still see their dear faces with the reddish frostbitten cheeks and ears, the light of the setting sun playing in their shiny sabre sheaths and silver harnesses, and smell the sweating horses. Since that day the melancholy yet pretty Russian folk songs remind me of that very last time I saw my dear regiment when they accompanied me to the Austrian station and said goodbye ... and yet now after over twenty years I still receive letters from these friends from the Akhtyrsky Regiment. It is scattered all over the globe but is still my regiment.

Grand Duchess Olga Alexandrovna in the Akhtyrsky uniform. She had been appointed Commander-in-Chief of this regiment on her wedding day in 1901.

Olga Alexandrovna to her niece Tatiana Nicholaievna

Lvov, 29th March 1915

My dear Tatiana,

How bad of me that I haven't written to you for such a long time, but you can be quite sure that the reason I do not write is not that I do not want to write - because I would like to write terribly often and tell you all a lot - but after rushing around all day, you get dreadfully tired, and when the day is finally over, you do not feel like writing and you forget anything interesting that you had intended to say. I have already written to Mama about Easter, so you know that. At 8 o'clock on the following morning I set out with eggs and presents for the whole Hospital* - and distributed the gifts - in the form of tobacco-pouches with all sorts of things in. *kissed everyone three times and said: Christ has risen! Risen indeed!

My precious Akhtyrskies are really dears. I dress their wounds myself every day. I do not leave that to anyone! My darlings Aglaimov and Ivan Susanin are very, very dear to me - and with them I can unburden my heart - in particular with dear Aglaimov - he is a real friend! If there is no more bandaging to do in the evening, I go over to sit with them in a small room - where the window is wide open, and we sit there together in the dusk and chat about life in general. Yesterday afternoon, we decided to go to the place where darling Guri Panaev had been killed. It is 30 versts from Lvov - he is buried in a churchyard in the village of Demnia - up above a large lake - it is a very nice place. We searched long for his grave - and in many other places we saw neglected graves - God's various forgotten children (slaves).....

My two lie next to each other - Guri and Nicholas Temperov have stone crosses and icons of the Akhtyrsky Mother of God... We stood there for a while, the three of us praying, and then we planted a willow and a flowering plant (which we had brought with us) and made crosses out of fir branches and adorned everything ... It was so sad - but joyous - since they were both nice and would have liked SUCH a death and they were so good that they are now surely in heaven with God.

On the whole – the Akhtyrskies are very spiritual people – even the boys, and with them it is easy to talk about pleasant things without being shy – they understand. Dear Aglaimov is simply incredibly good, and young. "Baby" Susanin is enormous and terribly dear as well. For Easter, I received many letters from the regiment and a telegram straight from the trenches. They had been involved in dreadful fighting again on Easter Day and that from six o'clock in the morning till ten o'clock at night – they had lost many men – and a whole infantry that was with them – two battalions surrendered (of course already extremely unfit for battle) and for them it was terribly painful. They had captured several machine guns and nevertheless pushed back the enemy out of the trenches – later they had to withdraw and – then there were losses...

Several light casualties arrived at the hospital and told us – but the heavily wounded stayed there.

So, on the second day – I was in a sad state because of it all.

Well that was that. I kiss you warmly just as much as I love you. There are so very many serious cases here – so that every day they die, and such wounds we have never seen before – what terrible horror. [In 1915 the Austro-Hungarian army began to use "Dum-Dum" bullets. The effect is that the bullet deforms and sometimes fragments upon impact, causing enormous lacerated wounds] .... There is a lot of work.

May God take care of you, my dear and everyone else, and I kiss Papa, Mama, Olga, Maria, Nastenka, Alyosha.

I love you, Aunt Olga

Source: GARF (Russian State Archives, Moscow)

CHAPTER 18

In the Line of Fire

*I*n *March 1915 our hospital was moved on to Lvov – Lemberg. We were all extremely pleased to go to a new place, and this one surpassed all expectations. We did, of course, arrive at the best time of year just as spring was setting in with all its glory. We spent Easter, which is the biggest event in the Greek Catholic Church, in this lovely town with its magnificent churches. We quickly became fond of this funny hilly town with its parks, its old buildings and Catholic churches and learnt how to find our way around in the beautiful surroundings. As soon as we had some free time, we would take ourselves for long walks out of town. The hillsides and woods were full of blue and white anemones, and I remember a pine forest where the undergrowth was all lovely pink pepper trees (Daphne), which had a scent like perfume. It was lovely everywhere we went, we had good working conditions, you could not ask for more... apart from peace of course, but that was naturally out of the question.*

Just before Easter two officers from my Akhtyrsky regiment were brought to our hospital. They were already on the way to recovery when they arrived so only had to spend their convalescence with us. They enjoyed their Easter holiday in the pleasant surroundings and regained their health quicker than one would have expected. When they were well enough to go out, they took me to see the battlefield, where the regiment had been in combat and where they had launched a cavalry attack. It had cost the regiment its colonel and seven of its best officers. They had been buried in a village churchyard next to a shattered belfry. We knelt by the graves of our friends, which was marked by a big white cross, and indulged in reminiscences.

Our stay in Lvov was not just spent going on excursions and walks. On the contrary, we were very busy. Towards the end of our time there, heavy fighting was going on at the front, and we were not so far away from it that we could always hear the canons thundering in the distance. New casualties were brought to us every single day – most of them were seriously wounded. It was a strenuous and nerve-racking work. We had a whole ward for soldiers with head injuries, which was the saddest to visit. Many of these poor sufferers were so seriously injured that they could not talk and quite a few died without us being able to identify them. In this ward it was usually deadly quiet, so quiet that it almost gave us a shock when a big fly crashed into one of the window panes with a bang. The weather was very hot, and only this buzzing sound and the voice of one poor fellow constantly calling one beloved name again and again broke the morbid silence. There was so little we could do to help him. It was in this ward that I really met the war in all its horror.

Here at Lvov my eldest brother visited us once more and helped to bring some cheer to these poor wounded souls. Shortly after, we were moved to a small place called Proskurov and there we spent the rest of that spring and summer. We were dreadfully sorry to leave Lvov, but Proskurov was a nice place to spend the summer in. It was only a small town, but it had some exceptionally lovely surroundings. To all sides, the golden cornfields waved in the wind like an ocean and there were big cool oak woods and lovely rivers and lakes. The place was in fact pretty. In Proskurov there was considerably less work for us than in Lvov, where we often had to work round the clock.

When we arrived in Proskurov, the barracks, where the hospital was to be housed, were not ready to be moved into, so we were accommodated in some empty carriages at the railway station. One day, to my great surprise, I happened to see the Colonel and two officers from my own regiment ride through town. I called out to them and if they weren't happy to see their honorary colonel, they at least pretended that they were. I must admit that I was very happy to see them. We spent some hours together, and when it was time to say goodbye, they asked if I would like to come with them to visit the regiment. It was stationed close to the front, less than a day's drive by car from Proskurov. I was given leave and joined them. We set out early one morning by motor car and reached the place late that afternoon. The road first took us through open flat country, through peaceful villages with white cottages, waving cornfields and beautiful dense woods. Then it took us to the town of Kamenetz-Podolsk, where a bridge spans a deep rocky valley. It was astounding to see this valley, which quite unexpectedly cuts its way through the flat surrounding countryside. Over on the other side we soon crossed the Austrian frontier. At about noon we could see hills in the distance. That was where the scene of battle had been. We drove on and reached the river Dnestr, which we had to cross over a narrow pontoon bridge at Zaleshchik. The original huge iron bridge had been shot to pieces and hung there like a distorted skeleton no longer spanning the river. As we approached the pontoon bridge, which naturally wasn't very wide, we joined a queue of carts filled with casualties, which we felt that we shouldn't overtake. As soon as we were over on the other side and had put some distance between us and this transport convoy, we were able to speed up again.

A bit further along, one of the officers insisted upon showing me the place where he had been wounded. We climbed a steep hill to the place and there he gave me a graphic account of what had happened. It was evident that we were standing on a battlefield. The ground was ploughed up by shells and there were big craters where they had dropped. If you hadn't been able to see this, you would have been able to smell that the place had been a battlefield. A nasty, sickly smell, characteristic of such places still clung to the field even though it had been months since there had been fighting in these parts. The officer also showed me how the seriously wounded had been carried and the lightly wounded dragged or slid down the steep hill to the road below, where the ambulances would be waiting.

After this stop we went back to our cars and continued our drive, but that was the end of driving fast. The road got worse and worse for each kilometre, and we often had to make long detours through the fields because the road had been shelled and had left deep holes full of muddy water. As we got near to the tiny deserted town of Snjiatin, we heard canons and suddenly saw a shell hit the earth in front of us. The officers gave me a sidelong glance to see how I was taking the experience, but I do not think that they noticed anything. For them it was nothing new. Close to the spot, where the shell had bored itself into the ground and sent a geyser of earth and stones up into the air, there was a soldier, who quite unruffled was breaking in a young horse. When we got closer, I recognized him as being one who had been a patient in my ward in Lvov. I waved to him. He first looked surprised, but then a look of recognition passed over his face and he waved back till the car was out of sight.

We continued driving for just under half an hour and finally reached our destination. When the regiment saw us arriving, the soldiers swarmed out of a number of cottages and gardens to bid us welcome. We shook hundreds of hands and were met with many happy smiles ... and then we went in search of suitable lodgings for an 'honorary colonel'. As the place had been deserted by the local population, it didn't take long till we found a small house ... it was a little pink and white two-roomed cottage. As soon as the soldiers saw where I was going to stay, they rolled up with their arms full of lilacs and other flowers and turned my room into a lovely bower of flowers, where I had a good night's sleep on a mattress on the floor. A soldier slept across the threshold in the next room and outside a comrade stood guard. I slept so well that I did not even hear when they relieved each other, but it had also been a strenuous day.

Next morning after breakfast quite a few of us walked through the deserted town, and climbed the church tower to have a look at the scene of battle. Our own batteries were positioned at the foot of the hill near the church. Far out in the distance we could see the enemy's batteries, which were busy firing.

Our officer's mess was in a cottage in the middle of an overgrown orchard not *far from the church. When the weather permitted, we would have our meals outside. One day, the divisional commander, General Gustav Mannerheim, arrived and spent part of the day with us. He was much loved by both officers and men for his calm and even character. While we were sitting at supper that first day in the orchard, I suddenly heard a thundering noise, which gave me the feeling that the top of my head would be carried off if I didn't hurry up and duck it – so I did that as quickly as I could – and a second later everyone burst out laughing at me. No one else had moved an inch. Then I heard a number of voices saying: 'never mind – we all did exactly what you did – the first time we were under fire'. For some time this deafening shooting continued both from our side and the enemy's batteries. It was an ear-deafening experience but somehow surprising how quickly you accustomed yourself to it. General Mannerheim suggested that we go somewhere else, but the officers answered that it would soon be dusk and then the enemy's 'evening salute' would stop. They were right.*

Later in the evening we heard that two of our gunners had been injured by enemy fire. We went out to look for them and found them in a clean little hospital where Catholic nuns were looking after them with much kindness. When the rest of the population had fled, these good women had stayed behind to continue their work of love and charity in that little town of Snjiatin.

Among the soldiers in my regiment was a young English volunteer. He had been an engineer in Russia when the war broke out. He first thought about returning to England, but being afraid that the war would be over before he had time to sign up, he enlisted in our army and ended up doing service in the Akhtyrsky Regiment. He did not speak very good Russian so was so pleased to speak English with me. I found out that he was an only son and was called Schack-Sommers. He talked about his plans for the future and about his father and mother, who he apparently loved deeply. A week later after I had returned to my Red Cross field hospital, I was told that he had been killed.

I spent one more day with the regiment – then they had to go somewhere else and under cover of darkness the whole force struck camp and moved to a big farm some distance away. There we again spent one more happy morning after which the regiment got marching orders, and I had to bid them farewell and return to my work.

Olga Alexandrovna to her niece Tatiana Nicholaievna

11th March, Kiev 1916

My darling Tatiana,

What are you doing? Anything nice?

We are very busy, and yesterday afternoon around 6 o'clock 50 men were brought to us. I washed them, scrubbed them and dressed them together with two other sisters and the wife of one of our medical attendants – 'Mme Sikorskaya'. In peacetime – the Sikorskaya couple were merchants.

We worked intensely for an hour and then carried them on stretchers – or some went on foot – upstairs and put them to bed and gave them supper. They had a good appetite! They were very hungry. Some had come straight from the trenches, others from the Proskurov hospital and Vinnitsa hospitals (Duma hospitals). They are all such dears but some are unhappy.

I have been working alone in our ambulance for quite a time now because a sister is ill with pleurisy and had to stay in bed for a long time. I was pleased that she was not here and that I had a lot of work so time passes quickly.

We are fasting and that is also calming and good. Again, I suddenly have the need to do a lot of sketching.

I have painted a big picture – the review of the regiment – i.e. a portrait of my dear commander astride his dappled horse – with the regiment marching past. Then I did pencil-drawings of the patients in a little album, then my room, views from different windows and so forth. Every day, a young doctor, who has already been here a year, reads aloud to me – and is happy to have me as a friend – although his nature is difficult and gloomy. We read many books. Quite a lot by Mereshkovski, then recently 'Judas Iskariot' by Andreev. It is interesting as a new idea. One day you will read it yourself. Well, and now we are again reading 'The Brothers Karamasov' by Dostoevsky. There at the beginning, there is a lot about old Zosim, and this goes well with the mood of our fasting.

My inside cannot digest vegetable oil, and yesterday I felt very ill. Tatiana Andreevna is so distressed that she has stopped writing. She is very worried and nervous about her sister – who has had many troubles in her life – and she writes a lot to her, and this pursuit takes up all her free time. She is now sitting near me and reading something. Sometimes I am terribly nervous and cannot sleep at all – otherwise, I manage fairly well.

The doctor says that I have a strong nature! Well – glory to God.

From time to time I go to Uncle Sandro for tea – however, he comes more often to us. For me it is really a pity not to have tea at home – I love all my family so much!

I particularly think about you on Saturdays; in my mind I am sitting with your mother on the bed and chatting with her, walking with Papa, sitting with you in your bedroom and smelling your perfume and I am there at night vespers...

Well my dear goodbye. God bless you!! I kiss you and embrace warmly and affectionately.

Always loving you, Aunt Olga.

Source: GARF (Russian State Archives, Moscow)

CHAPTER 19

My Greatest Wish

*I*n *August we were sent to Kiev which we were all very pleased about. It was good to be in that pretty town again. This time our hospital was installed in the big old building of a grammar school. It was a lovely spot with good working conditions. It was a long warm autumn that year of 1915, and Kiev looked wonderful with its old white churches and monasteries against the background of golden autumn leaves. We liked to get up very early and go for long walks, or sit on dewy benches in old parks or churchyards where we waited to see the sun rise. It was a marvellous sight when its first golden rays blended with the gold of the domes and crosses on the many churches. Then we would hurry back to our work in the hospital which began punctually at eight o'clock. It was also an interesting experience to go to the market in the morning which was always teeming with people. There we would help our matron to buy vegetables and provisions and carry them home. She was a dear old nurse and we all loved her. It was always easy to see when she was around as she was followed by numerous cats and dogs. They were normally to be found near her kitchen and did not want to run the risk of letting her go to the market on her own.*

I often wrote home and told my mother about our hospital and the beauty of Kiev which made her finally want to see everything herself. She was not disappointed. The first time she came she only stayed for two or three days. She lived in her carriage and went out and about during the daytime to visit hospitals and churches. Mother naturally came over to our hospital, and I was very proud to be able to show her in what a lovely and practical way we had organized it. She became so pleased with Kiev that when she left, she said: 'I shall soon return again'. This she did. In most large Russian towns there is a so-called 'palace', and my mother took possession of the one in Kiev when she came back and spent about ten months there. She often visited the hospitals and was a welcome guest at many estates in the neighbourhood. Not only did Mother have her own motorcar at her disposal, but she also had a small steamer which she frequently used on the River Dnieper which is one of the main thoroughfares in Kiev.

The palace was situated in a big shady park on the high bank of the river. From it there was such a lovely view of the broad Dnieper and the forests which stretched out on the other side. My eldest brother, the Emperor, came to Kiev right

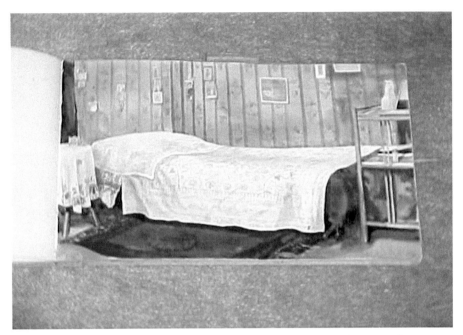

Watercolour by Grand Duchess Olga Alexandrovna of her bedroom in her Kiev hospital, February 20th, 1916.

at the beginning of November bringing his son, Alexei, with him. He was now a handsome tall boy of almost thirteen and charmed everyone. One day he visited our hospital and that day all our nurses lost their hearts to him. Being his paternal aunt I was very proud and happy. It was unfortunate that I couldn't spend as much time with my brother and Alexei as I would have liked to, but I had a nasty boil in my throat. That visit was incidentally the last time I saw my brother and his boy. In the course of this visit I had a long cherished wish granted: I was given my brother's permission and blessing to marry the love of my youth, the young cavalry officer Kulikovsky.

When I look back at the three years I worked as a hospital nurse I have the feeling that I did a useful piece of work. I opened up my heart wide to our brave dear soldiers who were like big children, and in the course of the years I have received much evidence that they were just a little fond of me too. The work was hard, but it was a task that first and foremost taught me something about the human soul – particularly in times of war. Again and again I witnessed how many different ways the soul follows out of this life and into eternity.

I remember so many deaths where there were awful struggles, and many

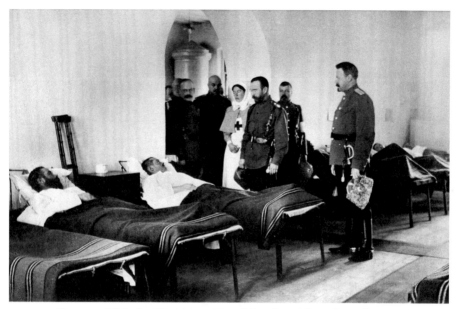

Emperor Nicholas II visiting Grand Duchess Olga Alexandrovna's hospital in Kiev 1916.

tears were shed. But one of the first deaths I experienced as a nurse turned out to be so calm and beautiful as if it had been a sunset. The young soldier who was about to die had been an assistant in a big shop before the war. Now he was seriously injured and his body had already started to putrefy. There was no hope for him. One morning, when I arrived at his sickbed he was lying there on some pillows which had been piled up so high that he was almost sitting. He was very pale and had his eyes closed. When he heard me coming he opened them for a moment, looked at me and tried to smile. I stood at his bed for a while and tried to warm his cold white hands in mine. Suddenly, the expression on his face changed. He smiled so peacefully and happily and whispered quite softly: 'Sister, can you hear the church bells ringing? How beautiful they are!' I could not hear a thing but couldn't bring myself to say so. Then he whispered: 'Could you please open the window so that I can hear the bells better?' I hastened to fulfil his wish. When I returned to his bed, he was lying there quite peacefully with the same happy expression and said: 'What a lovely sunset ... it is so delightful ... and then those bells!' He sighed deeply – not grumbling, but just content – and then it was over. His face had stiffened into this happy expression similar to when you have seen something wonderfully beautiful. I am sure that he had.

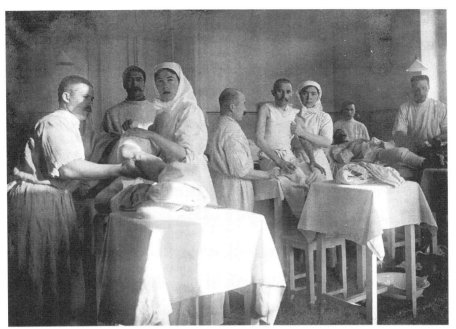

Grand Duchess Olga Alexandrovna as a Red Cross nurse in Kiev, 1916.

At a certain time, we had many wounded Austrians in our hospital. They were so friendly and polite, and we so pitied these poor souls who were not only wounded but had to spend their stay in hospital far away from home, family and friends. On one particular day, many Austrians were admitted to the hospital. Many of them were seriously injured, but none of them uttered a single sound while their wounds were being dressed. From the very first day I immediately noticed a young Austrian who had actually only been lightly wounded. He had been shot in the underarm just above his wrist, but since the injury had not looked serious no one had taken the trouble to clean the wound properly and the result was that blood poisoning had affected the whole of his right arm. His hand and arm had turned black right up to his shoulder and there wasn't much hope of saving his life. He sat there in his bed looking sadly at his black right hand which really wasn't his any more. He pointed at his wedding ring and told me that he had been married just as the war had broken out and that now his wife was expecting a baby. He lifted his poor hand up with the other arm and kissed the ring and shook his handsome head in despair. There was only one thing to do: we had to try to amputate his arm. We did, but it was too late. The inflammation had already spread too far.

*Grand Duchess Olga
Alexandrovna and Nicholas
Kulikovsky on their wedding day,
November 4th, 1916.*

On the morning after the operation he was only semi-conscious. He lay there quite still in his white bed only waiting for his dear little wife to visit him. Each time I approached his bed, he asked me: 'Hasn't my wife arrived yet?' and at the same time the tears trickled down on his wedding ring which he was holding in his left hand, so that he could still see it He became weaker and weaker and was quickly slipping away. But to the very last minute he lay there with his big blue, feverish eyes staring at the door where he hoped to see his loved one. I do not think that he expected to survive for a second but was just hoping to see her again for the very last time, to hear her voice and feel her hand through his hair. It was almost unbearable to watch. The last time I went into his ward, he suddenly cried out: 'But, there you are, my own love ... at long last you have come!' And then he died with a deep, happy sigh, which proved that he had indeed met his little beloved wife for the last time. Love is stronger than death.

On November 5th / 17th my present husband and I were married in the oldest church that exists in Russia. It had been built on the spot where there had previously stood a wooden image of the heathen god 'Perun'. When Kiev became Christian the inhabitants had thrown this figure down the hill into the Dnieper, and had founded the first church on the spot where it had stood for such a long time. It was snowing hard on the day we were married. My brother-in-law drove me to church, and my mother followed in the next car with one of my favourite nurses. There were only a few guests in the church. Apart from them, only my mother's Cossack bodyguard Yachik, the colonel from my own regiment and one officer were present. The church lay in darkness except for the spot where we stood and where light fell from the candles. Up on the gallery a choir sang very beautifully filling the old church with their voices. After the ceremony we drove back to the hospital and all had dinner together. All my comrades, the doctors and nurses were so pleased for me and wished us happiness with all their hearts. We were so happy. Thus our greatest wish for thirteen years had been fulfilled. After the wedding we were both given a fortnight's leave. We spent that time in the home of one of my husband's childhood friends. The two of them had been neighbours. True enough, their parents' farms had been situated about 30 km from each other, but that had not been considered a problem. They were not just neighbours, but 'close' neighbours and the two families would often have lunch or dinner together and drive home afterwards without giving a thought to the distance. When we arrived at the house the whole of the large family was gone, with the exception of a lady in her early thirties who took care of the household all on her own. She bade us welcome and told us to make ourselves at home – and that was what we did. It was a cosy old farmhouse with massive, old-fashioned furniture, hand-woven tablecloths and carpets which had belonged to the family for generations. Our hostess thought that I was so thin and run down, so she fed me from morning to night on the most delicious and nourishing country fare.

We had a lovely time in these peaceful surroundings. They made us completely forget that a war was raging out in the world. There was a cosy smell of burning wood and dogs in the house. The countless 'greyhounds' had the free run of the whole house and considered it as interference in their private rights if anyone was to sit on the settees and chairs, where they were used to settling down. After lunch we would go out for sleigh rides to those places which held so many memories for my husband. We called on the neighbours – and they came over to us for tea. The days passed much too quickly.

After a lovely twelve-day honeymoon, we had to leave this cosy spot where we had been able to hide from the world and all its concerns. On the way to Kiev we stopped for a day in Kharkov where my husband's mother and grandmother lived. The grandmother had never seen me before and made me feel quite awkward when she took me by the shoulders and turned me towards the light so that her weak eyes could see me better. And when she had done that she said: 'I wanted to have a decent impression of what you look like before I go quite blind'. She was a tall and burly old lady who had a mind of her own, and a strong will which she compelled everyone to respect. 'Grandmother' lived in a big, old house which she owned herself and where there were loads of paintings and family portraits. My mother-in-law was a dear and loving lady, and I took an immediate liking to her. We didn't really get closely acquainted till we later sought refuge in the same Cossack town, and there we grew incredibly fond of each other. Perhaps I had best just answer for myself, but I am quite convinced that she also liked me even though we both loved the same man.

Olga Alexandrovna to Tatiana Nicholaievna

4th November Kiev, 1916

My dear darling Tatiana

It seems that I haven't written to you for a long time! Your hand-writing is in such huge letters that there are very few words on each page. Well, it looks like I will have to tell you off. This morning, when I saw something printed about me in the newspaper, I got terribly confused – I read it while I was having coffee – but then I got used to this new thought – and cannot say enough how my soul was unburdened – as if it was a celebration for me [the Grand Duchess Olga Alexandrovna was wedded to Captain Nicholas Kulikovsky)! The sisters did not say anything to me, but in the evening I found five pots of flowers in my room and then I felt embarrassed when I thanked them – several soldiers said some touching words from them all and that they were happy for me, that they loved me and wished me all the best. Today a former cuirassier came to me – young captain Kvasn – who was in Uncle Misha's regiment last year. Now he is a Cossack officer in the Kabardian Regiment. I naturally addressed him in the familiar term as before – and then when he said goodbye before leaving – he suddenly said to me: "I have read about you in the newspaper and I am very happy for you – may God grant you prosperity and happiness in your new life". I was amazed by this!...

Uncle George has arrived here – he spent an hour with me yesterday, asked for tea – but although there is a samovar at this hour in the corridor – it was not "tea-time" – so I brought him the leftovers of a roll, jam and a tea-glass – he wasn't exactly pleased – teased me and laughed loudly! All the same, he seems to be the kindest of all the brothers – but I wouldn't want to be his wife!

Four of us had dinner with Grandmother, him, Sandro and I. There were not more than 30 to have their dressings changed in our ambulance – and in another one – next to this one. That is very little. It is warm here as if it were summer. About fourteen degrees in the shade – it is sunny and from time to time there are "showers". There is a lot of beauty in the autumnal colouring of the leaves. I do a little sketching.

We recently went to the cinema and saw something very interesting. "The Portrait of the Countess" or "The Mystery of the old Castle".

It was how a young tutor came to the three year old son of the Count (unfortunately – in German). The Count is old – all he wants to do is to go hunting – and his young wife is, of course, absorbed in the tutor, and then it turned out that they had been introduced to each other and fallen in love three hundred years ago in the same castle – and the tutor knew all about what had happened from the portrait – which hung in his cheerless room and came out of the frame in the night and forced him to read the old manuscripts – which were stored in his room in a secret box. Then it was evident how they had lived earlier – and that he had been a troubadour – and they had been caught and he had been executed ... He (i.e. the tutor) – being a sensible German – listens to the admonitions of the portrait – and it is not too late – so he escapes from the castle! ...It was very lovely and interesting – not quite like I wrote of course!... And then another – dreadfully sad and beautiful film – "For a Moment of Happiness" – from present day life in France. A regiment happened to be stationed on an estate, and a handsome young officer naturally falls in love with the young daughter. She was consumptive – and finally when they were given permission to marry (by then he had been wounded and she was taking care of him) – she died after some days in his arms... Dreadful how sad it was. ....I cried quietly under a big flat black hat (the hat of Emma Ivanova) so that the people next to me couldn't see ...

I haven't seen N.A. for more than two months, but this isn't so sad since I know where he is and no longer shake in the night thinking about the war etc.

God bless you, my darling Tatiana. I kiss you and everyone else very, very dearly.

I love you, your Aunt Olga

Source: GARF (Russian State Archives, Moscow)

Olga Alexandrovna to Nicholas II

[Written in English with an exact transcription]

10th November, 1916 in Podgornoye

Good morning, Nicky-darling.

It isn't yet a week since we are married & but 5 days that we are here in the country. I'll tell you now about the wedding day, which was awfully nice. The day before, your Mama announced her wish to be present (which touched me awfully) and at the same time she was awfully deranged because she didn't want the police or "Micha Evald" (probably a playful code word for plain clothes men) to follow her there. This question was seen to by Sandro who went & invited the Governor & told him that not one policeman was to be placed anywhere near the Church, & then Mama drove to tea to Sandro's house and from there they came to fetch the bride ... Meantime I was dressed & coiffed by Amalia Ivanovna & all the 19 sisters squeezed into the room to watch this proceeding. I had a wreath of orange-blossom and a veil on my head. All the way to Church in the motor Mama was seized with tremendous fourires [sic] and kept asking Tatiana Andreevna "Where are we going?" To which the latter only crossed herself with a delighted face & answered, "Glory to God, Glory to God."

N[icholas] A[lexandrovich] with commander Eltyaninov (his best man) t(w)o officers and one doctor (Pupka), the chauffeur, all drove just in front of us and we all entered the old lovely church in a bunch.

The Church is called Kiev Vasily Church, near the monument of the holy Olga on Tryokhsviyatitel Street, on the spot where stood the statue of Perun [the old Russian god of thunder]. I chose this old Church because it is out of the way & because it is old & pretty, not big, very high & dark. The old priest too is a very sympathetic old man & we went to Holy Communion the day before. He calls one "my child" and "thou", which makes one feel cozy at once & spoke awfully nicely when I spoke of my divorce. He was awfully frightened to see Mama & though it was very cold in Church, he had big beads of perspiration on his face when he met her. There was a splendid choir which sang the "God have mercy" I like, with one voice which soars high up in the sky like a lark, you know.

The snow was falling outside all the afternoon. Sandro & Eltyaninov told us that once during the service an old general entered the Church & thinking it was a simple vsyenosnaya (evening prayer), pulled off his cap & shook the snow from it & his coat, but just as he was making himself ready to pray, he heard the words: "here the slave of God, Grand Duchess Olga Alexandrovna, is married to the slave of God Nicholas, in the name of the Father, of the Son , and of the Holy Spirit..." looked up terrified & rushed out of Church!.... Dear Yachik [Marie Feodorovna's Cossack bodyguard] stood in a corner also.

When the service was over, the old priest shook our hands warmly & took us to the door & said lots of kind words. This time the couple was put into a motor alone & it all seemed too beautiful to be true. At the hospital door we were met by all the sisters & doctors who threw hops and oats at us & flew round our necks. On the stairs stood all the wounded who could walk. Mama & Sandro remained to supper & it was all so awfully nice & cosy. Andreyevsky the manager & the apothecary made some impossible "fruit wine" and very soon I saw that nearly all the Co. were slightly fuddled!

At about 8 Mama, Sandro & the Akhtyrskies [soldiers of the regiment for which Olga was patroness] left us, & then the Co. went mad! One of the doctors played the piano and the others all danced (I also). The young black doctor, who had drunk a drop too much, was killing! He danced, rocked about & fell over the chairs & onto the tables, when we all laughed he explained, "I am not at all drunk; I just have a poor heart and cannot stand dancing for a longer time." ... At last the poor boy was found on my bed feeling very ill! So he was coaxed with great difficulty, to get up & go upstairs to the guardroom (he was a guard too) there he spent the rest of the evening being sick into a sky-blue enamel pot, while a sister, who is very fond of him, sat by his side changing a wet towel on his chest and stroking his head. When we ran up to say goodbye to him, he kissed us both lovingly, again assured me he was not a bit tipsy, and absently kissed my husband's hand.

Then we said goodbye to all the Co. & some begged me to come back in 2 weeks, others asked me to remain away & rest for a month ....

and we drove to the station. There in the wagon we found 5 Akhtyrskies, who came to wish us good things; & our friend little Atylaimov (my chauffeur) came with us to Kursk.

Here there is very little snow, 18 versts from the station Podgornoye and a drive across steppes. Very little woods or water. The house we live in is rather big & belonged to, once upon a time, to a chairman of the nobility Lutovinov, now it belongs to his daughter an old maid of 39, very sympathetic, jolly, simple and who does everything about her estate herself, like a man. She lives alone with an old & cosy housekeeper called Feodosia Vasilyevna, whose one goal for the present moment is to fatten me up. She eats with us at table, sits opposite me & counts every mouthful. Any amount of dogs and cats sit on every sofa & armchair, terrible dramas take place daily, as the black cat came home with a terrible tooth abscess & the other cat will probably get eat up one of these days...

Every morning N.A. & I drive over to our piece of land (800 deshatin [1 deshatina = 1.09 hectares] a nice place: hills & valleys, all covered with oak trees, very pretty & every day we run about & find splendid places, on which we think of building our house. The house we have bought, and when the snow falls, we shall have it brought here & put up. Here one does such things, all the time, buys someone's house, takes it to pieces, and puts it up on ones own estate.

Yesterday we had the local chairman of the nobility with his young wife, to tea & supper (also he is a friend of N.A. & the mistress of this house, since they were all children together). Golostenov he is called, very sympathetic. Today our friend the priest from Zivopisnoye (near Ramon) came to spend some days. He is awfully nice & we want him to get back here.

By the way, I beg your pardon by telegraphing about the permission to get married, because I was awfully afraid it would come too late, as I told you Saturday, & then only found out that Saturdays one can't get married.

Nicky dear I can't tell you how I thank you for everything. It is so marvellous & I am so happy! I was also very disappointed not to be able to speak to you alone when you came to us at Kiev.

Perhaps you'll send this letter on to Alix, because I am tremendously lazy and can't write all this over again and I want to write to her, so if you can please do, & save me the trouble of writing everything again. Here we go to bed at 8½ or 9 o. as it is very dark, only one small Kerosene lamp in the room (as one can't get any, so it is economic not to burn much) so it is difficult to write or read & in the day time we are out much.

Natalia Andreevna, dear soul, was so excited & delighted at our marriage that she cried & laughed & even danced "Russian."

Now I must stop. God bless you darling Nicky dear. I hug you and your son; I got a delightful & touching letter from my friend Nikita, upon my wedding, too killing & sincere.

From your loving old sister

Olga

Source: GARF (Russian State Archives, Moscow)

Countess Zinaide Mengden*: The Empress Marie Feodorovna in Kiev. 1916/1917.

On 1st May 1916 we went to Kiev again. It was the intention that we would also this time be staying there for about fourteen days. Little did we know that we would never again return to Petrograd. In Kiev we stayed at the palace which is situated in a beautiful and high position and enjoys an extensive view of the Dnieper River... When the Empress drove out on her daily trips she did not like to have her retinue with her. But Kiev's Governor, Alexei Ignatiev, and a police officer did not abstain from driving after the Imperial automobile at such a distance that the Empress was not aware of them.

Source: "The Memoirs of the Countess Zinaide Mengden*", pages 92–93

CHAPTER 20

The Flight to the Crimea

*T*he news that a revolution had broken out in St. Petersburg came to those of us who worked in our hospital in Kiev like a veritable thunderbolt. We hadn't heard a word – not even a rumour, but one morning it was all over the newspapers. We read the news over and over again and did not want to believe our eyes. Our patients were just as surprised and terrified as we were ourselves. They stared at us with bewildered eyes, and couldn't stop asking what would become of them and the rest of us. We hadn't a notion and barely knew what had happened. None of us could foresee how much it would disrupt all our lives.

My Mother immediately set off by train to the headquarters at Moghilev to see and speak with her eldest son, the Emperor. It was a trying journey for her … and it would have been many times more trying if she had known that it would be the last time she would be seeing Nicky.

While Mother was away, the general mood in Kiev slowly changed. It was evident that the revolution was on the way. We discussed the situation and realised that we had to change our whereabouts. As soon as Mother returned to Kiev my brother-in-law, Xenia's husband, suggested that we take her as far away as possible from the danger spot. We should take her to the Crimea where he owned an estate named Ai-Todor. It was situated on the Black Sea and here he believed that we would be in safety. He had already given his wife and children instructions to leave St. Petersburg and travel to the Crimea to join us there as quickly as they possibly could.

The next problem turned out to be how to get down there. The ordinary train connections were highly unreliable, but then with great efforts and through private connections my brother-in-law succeeded in procuring a special train which was made ready for immediate departure. My husband and I decided to accompany Mother and the others to the Crimea, but we intended to return immediately to our duties as soon as the whole family had been installed in their temporary home. And then off we went. We set out late one night, but it was not from the station where it would have caused a commotion and where hundreds of helpless people were waiting for an opportunity to get away, but from a small wood a short distance from Kiev. We drove out there in the dark, found the train at the appointed spot, got in and away it immediately puffed. We were on our way for two days *and stopped at a number of major stations. There our escort of a few soldiers stood at all the doors to prevent the wagons from being taken by storm by the crowds of demoralized people, who had decided to fish in troubled waters and who were waiting for an opportunity to get somewhere else where there was something going on. Thankfully, the journey went as planned, despite the many difficulties. All traffic was in a great state of chaos and we had the feeling that we were just waiting for our train to crash into another one which had been left on the tracks, because the staff could not agree to man it and drive it away. We still cannot really understand how our train avoided accidents and got through safely. It was such an emotional journey. As we approached Sevastopol the train slowed down and stopped at a previously arranged spot some distance from town. There some motorcars were waiting to drive us along the picturesque mountain road – some three hours' drive – to our destination Ai-Todor.*

Under normal circumstances this drive to Ai-Todor would have been a wonderful experience. At first, the road takes you over rocky heights and climbs kilometre after kilometre, then one comes to a bend in the road and after a short tunnel one looks out over a beautiful panorama, with the Black Sea spread out in front of you. Its dark waters would glitter so much in the sunshine that your eyes almost started hurting. The sky, which arches over this beautiful view, is as deep-blue as in the Mediterranean countries and the air is clean and light as if it were charged with health. When you have had your fill of the beautiful view you start looking for the road which winds its way down the mountainside between rocks, trees and vineyards. After this, the road almost runs horizontally high above the blue waves of the Black Sea, and then you are in Ai-Todor.

After we had been there for three days we slowly started wondering what had become of Xenia and her children, but then they turned up safe and sound after a smooth though arduous journey from St. Petersburg. For the first week or so life seemed quiet and normal. We had the feeling that we had avoided a dreadful storm, and were in safety in our little cosy nook far away from the centre where the revolution was boiling. My mother and my sister would drive out or go for walks and enjoyed the early warm spring sunshine, which was especially early arriving that year as if it felt that we were in extra need of comfort. After a while our tingling nerves started to calm down. In March the chestnut trees were in bloom and wild yellow crocuses pushed their heads up between the stones. It was spring everywhere you looked. The only thing that worried us was the thought of my eldest brother and his family. We wished many a time that we had had them with us. *The house wasn't particularly big but we shared it as best as we could. My husband and I lived in a room downstairs next to one of my nephews.*

Mother, her maid and my eldest nephew lived upstairs. The rest of the family had moved over to the old house nearby.

But unrest also found its way to our little refuge. One night we were awakened by a violent knocking at our door – then it was opened and we heard the rattling of arms while a voice said: 'Keep quiet and please put your hands on top of the blanket'. A sailor armed to the teeth stepped in, shut the door behind him and said: 'In the name of the Provisional Government you are not permitted to leave this room!' We were much too astonished at first to say anything so just lay there staring at this heavily armed guard. He didn't say a word but sank down onto a sofa opposite us and leaned his head against his rifle barrel. This is how he sat for a while. There was dead silence in the room. Suddenly, he said in a subdued whisper – almost as if he was thinking aloud: 'If I were you I would get up and put on some clothes. Never mind my presence, I'll shut my eyes.' We took his advice little thinking that we would have to spend five hours together!!

For a while no one said a word, but then little by little we began to talk with our guard who answered in a friendly manner. That was how we found out that a ship had come from Sevastopol, with an expeditionary force on board, in order to track down a 'secret radio station' that the government believed was installed at Ai-Todor. Apart from that they also had to search for a huge secret reserve of arms which we were supposedly hiding. The whole force was armed to the teeth which was more than clear from the arms the guard was equipped with. He told us that the sailors had been informed by their commanders that they would be going on an extremely dangerous mission. By now, our sailor-guard could surely understand that there was no major risk for life and limb, and casting a glance round the room he looked at us and added: 'If I had only known the sort of expedition we would be going on, believe me, I would never have volunteered!' The poor man was completely worn out. He had not slept the whole night, and was dead-tired from the long march up from the port at Yalta to Ai-Todor. He was a sailor and not accustomed to marching – and not the least with heavyweight equipment. It all ended up with him falling asleep again and again.

In one of his waking moments we asked him what was going on in the house. He answered thin-lipped: 'perquisition – a house search!' And then he added: 'They will soon be down here; then you'll be pleased that I made you get up and dress. Your bed and everything in it will be turned inside out whether you are in it or not. You've got nothing to hide, have you?' No, we certainly did not have. The hours passed, and there was still no sign of an inspection. We even started to assume that we would be spared further questioning, but then at about 10 o'clock a whole crowd suddenly appeared. It consisted of many heavily armed sailors and some workmen.

Our particular guard jumped up and told his comrades, the sailors, that he was responsible for the room and that they should disappear immediately. At the same time he proceeded to prod the ones in front in the stomach with his gun and most energetically hustled them all out. Then the workmen started their work and they did it thoroughly. They pulled every single drawer out and spread the contents over the floor. They turned the bed upside down, pulled the window blinds up and down, rolled up the carpet to see if anything was hidden under it, ripped open the sofa cushions so the feathers flew all over the place and made a fine mess. It was all for nothing as we had nothing of any interest to them. Then they disappeared again leaving the room in a wild disorder.

The expeditionary force had arrived early in the morning, and their inspection had lasted way into the afternoon. During all this time none of us had had anything to eat or drink so we were very hungry. Our 'guardians' had not had anything to eat either and were just as hungry as we were. Someone was sent for bread and cheese, and meanwhile nearly all the sailors flung themselves down on the green grass under our windows and went immediately to sleep – and that wasn't exactly noiselessly! For as long as the sailors were in the grounds of the property we were not allowed to leave our respective rooms, so it was not till they had left in the late afternoon that we could hurry upstairs to find out how my mother and the others had fared during that eventful day. Our mother's two rooms had been rummaged most and were in a dreadful state. The unwelcome guests had taken all her letters, her Danish bible, all her photographs, even those with the smallest inscription on, flung them into a big sack and taken everything away. Mother did not seem in the least bit tired but she was boiling with indignation at how she had been treated, and had given them all quite a piece of her mind which certainly had not made matters any better! Mama's maid was in tears and had heard her calling for her, but had been unable to run to her help.

After we had all related our experiences, vented our rage and discovered that no major damage had been done, we took the whole affair with good humour and somehow tried to laugh. Our appetites returned together with our good spirits. We were all dreadfully hungry, but it was difficult to satisfy it as our guests had taken and eaten everything and left a bare pantry. After such an eventful day we had all looked forward to a bite of food, and it was such a disappointment that our 'guests' had not given their hosts the slightest thought.

Countess Zinaide Mengden*: Moghilev, the Flight to the Crimea 1917.

In the evening of the 3rd of March, the Empress took the Princes Schervaschidze, Dolgoruky and me to Moghilev, the General Headquarters. She was accompanied by her son-in-law Alexander Michaelovitch, who was in charge of the trip...

On the 9th of March at five o'clock in the afternoon we went back to Kiev. Here everything had changed while we had been away. There was not the customary reception at the station, the governor of the town had not appeared and no Cossacks stood at the carriage door ...

On the 11th of March the Empress told me that her son-in-law, Grand Duke Alexander had suggested to her that the two of them go to the Crimea together and leave their suites behind. That the Empress refused to do .... Finally, the Empress decided to go to the Crimea but only with her suite.

On 23rd March she gathered all the officers on duty for a luncheon in order to bid them farewell. After first having been to a service in Kiev in the Michael abbey church for the last time, we left the town in the evening at half past seven and headed for the Crimea...
Our travel group consisted of the Empress with her entourage, namely Prince Dolgoruky and his wife, me, Grand Duchess Olga and her husband, Grand Duke Alexander and his attendant, General Fogel, and the two loyal Cossack bodyguards Yachik and Poliakoff and the servants. Prince Schervaschidze stayed behind in order to go to Petrograd to see to the Dowager Empress's affairs. He joined us later in the Crimea ...

On the 25th March we arrived at the station in Inkerman, where we got out of the train to continue the journey by automobile till we reached the Crimea where the Ai-Todor estate is situated on the Black Sea. During her stay there, the Empress lived in a roomy villa, which was called "The New House". Grand Duke Alexander and his family had a somewhat bigger and older house, which was completely covered in creepers and where the most wonderful bunches of grapes peeped out here, there and everywhere. The two buildings were situated opposite each other on a hill; a little further down there was a house, the so-called "Suite House", where all those of us lived who made up the suite ...

On the 26th of April my maid woke me up at half past five in the morning. She told me that the house was surrounded by sailors, who had thrown pebbles at her window to wake her up.

Source: "The Memoirs of the Countess Zinaide Mengden"*, pages 104, 108–112

CHAPTER 21

A Roll-Call

*A*fter the Sevastopol-Soviet had made their house search at Ai-Todor, we were *so to say confined to the estate 'for our own safety's sake'. The sailors stayed in the grounds and stood guard at the gates. No one could enter or leave without asking their permission.*

The spring with all its beauty passed without giving a thought to all the horror that was going on in the world. Then the hot, dry summer came bringing with it the greatest joy of my life: our eldest son was born one August evening. I naturally loved him from the very first day with a love only a mother can give, and he was, of course, to become everyone's ray of sunshine. Many hours, which else would have appeared quite long, passed caring for this young gentleman and playing with him. We sewed and knitted clothes for him. He lay in the same cradle as all his cousins had once done. His pram was an antediluvian thing of the past. We watched over him day and night, never left him for a second and had him with us wherever we went. He was so precious.

We had enough to eat although we were short of coffee and tea from time to time, but we managed. We would go into the woods and pick up acorns and make coffee out of them. Tea we made out of dried hips from the garden. Everyone who came for a visit told us how tasty it was. For us in the Ai-Todor colony the present substitutes do not offer many major surprises! After my son was born, the three of us moved over to small lodgings in a house over my brother-in-law's wine-cellar. It was a lovely spot. The house was situated just above the vineyards and what a lovely view it was across them to the sea beyond. In the evening when the air got cooler we would often sit on our balcony and admire the sunset. Then the twilight would change quickly into southern darkness, and the bluish evening sky with its golden clouds into a black velvet blanket which had become alive with glittering stars. Despite all this beauty, there was no real peace in our hearts. Everything was so uncertain and we never saw a newspaper, but the air was full of rumours and they were all most discouraging. It is not surprising that it was sometimes difficult to keep up one's spirits. Added to all this, it gradually became most difficult to get provisions of any kind. None of us had any money and it went so far that we couldn't even pay our servants the salaries that were due to them. Under such circumstances we were immensely touched that they stayed with us all the same, and that purely out of kindness and devotion. I really do not know how we would have managed without them – none of us were used to heavy housework.

Strangely enough, I kept receiving nice letters from my comrades at the hospital in Kiev. They wrote that our hospital had been shut like all the other ones, and that there was nothing for them to do. They had tried to get to the North (St. Petersburg), but there were no trains running there, and now three of them were asking if they could come and visit us for a few days instead. Trains were still running south even though they were mostly unpunctual. They were, of course, most welcome, and one dark evening they reached Ai-Todor. When they arrived at the entrance gate they were stopped by the sailor on guard who asked them what they wanted. After they had explained their business he accompanied them to our lodgings, hammered at the door, opened it and asked with a twinkle in his eye: 'Do you know these women?' I had no time to answer as I was nearly suffocated in their warm embraces! My three girl friends did not come alone. They had been somewhat uneasy about the long journey so had asked one of their friends to accompany them. Young Mr. Thal worked for the Red Cross and was a most enthusiastic mountaineer. Since he had never had an opportunity to climb mountains in the Crimea he had eagerly seized the opportunity to go there for a few days. We found lodgings for them and met for lunch the following day. During the meal the young man talked happily about a long climb he wanted to do up to the highest point of the mountains – Ai-Petri – that towered above us just behind the estate. He wanted to set out the following morning.

The next morning we were up early to see him off. Beaming with happiness he went on his way, turned round a couple of times and waved to us. That was the last we saw of him. He disappeared without a trace. Several search parties were fitted out to find him – dead or alive – but they were all in vain. Somewhat later, his poor father arrived and spent a lot of money sending out a party to find his son or at least his body, but he was well and truly gone. Nothing was ever heard of him again. My 'war comrades' as I called my girl friends were naturally awfully saddened by this tragedy. Their stay in the Crimea which we had all so looked forward to, had been quite spoilt.

One fine spring morning in February 1918 a group of strange-looking people suddenly arrived at the estate. They scowled at us, pulled out a long list of names and ordered everyone – beginning with my mother and ending with the cook – to file past them one by one as their names were called out and which were then crossed off on the list.

Mother was indignant at their behaviour and refused to obey orders for a long time. No one could persuade her to show herself. Finally, she understood that it *would be worse if these 'gentlemen' were to force their way into her rooms. When she finally opened her door and looked down over the banister a rough voice called out 'Maria Romanov' and crossed her name off. We were all standing there on the landing. To our horror we then heard Mama call back: 'You have forgotten to put my dog's name on the list!'*

My husband and I were most astonished that our names were not on the list. After the roll-call was over we asked why we hadn't been 'counted', and were told that we were not on the list because I was married to an ordinary man. We were free and could go where we liked. This was just as incomprehensible as so many other things that happened in those days!!! At the same time, we were informed that everyone on the list would be moved somewhere else the following day and had to get ready to leave. After a hurried packing the following morning my mother, sister, all her family, all their staff and servants were shut up in the house of Grand Duke Peter – the brother of Grand Duke Nicholas Nicholaievich. They and their families and staff had already been confined there. Djulber was not even a large house and had only been built for one family. The building was in Moorish style and had a high white wall running along three sides of it, right down to the sea. Probably, this wall had attracted attention and therefore this place was made into a prison – easy to guard and difficult to escape from.

As we saw them being driven off, our hearts were very heavy. My husband, our son and I were now alone at Ai-Todor. We thought a little about staying where we were but realised that we did not wish to remain in the forsaken and empty Ai-Todor where there were so many memories, so we decided to move on. We wanted to be as close as possible to the others and found two small rooms not too far from Djulber, and there we settled down with our two old maids and the baby of six months. We were not allowed to visit Mother and the family, but sometimes in the morning we would climb the mountainside from whence we could look down and see the 'prisoners' walking in the garden of Djulber. We would wave our hands and sometimes they would see us and wave an answer. Then we would go home happy and comforted.

The winter passed and spring came round once again. Nature was just as wonderful as it always is. It was so warm, so sunny and the sea glittered beautifully again. Flowers in magnificent colours, which one only finds in the South, surged up between the rocks on the mountainside. There were spots where peonies grew in profusion. Close to them was the source of a small stream where primroses grew in big tufts of yellow or pink and covered the moist earth. In other places magnolia trees spread their fresh scent into the air, and large bright pink trees called 'Judas' trees made splashes of colour among the green foliage. The birds sang happily – nature was jubilant – what a contrast to everything that was going on around us. The air was thick with dreadful rumours which unfortunately became certainties. We were surrounded by chaos and anarchy. Everyone was uncertain and afraid of everyone else – you could not trust anyone but yourself. So many innocent people were ruthlessly murdered in their homes or on public roads. No one would intervene. It was an awful spring.

One day we saw a destroyer sail past us on its way to Yalta – about ten kilometres away. We saw it stop there and open fire on the town without the slightest reason. The shooting continued for two days and only stopped at lunchtime and at night. Then it stopped and the ship sailed off again as suddenly as it had arrived. No one knew where it had come from, who it had on board, why there had been shooting and where it sailed off to. It was just there! Another day we saw an unknown merchant ship appear in the waters near the lighthouse of Ai-Todor. Suddenly, a battery close by on shore started firing at the ship, and we could see how the shells fell around it into the sea. It had apparently not had any bad intentions, but it had not been summoned so had to turn and fly!

At such a troubled time life naturally looked very bleak for our prisoners at Djulber. It is quite possible though that the uncertain conditions were of advantage to my mother and the rest of the family, and that their prison guards felt somewhat isolated so far away from their 'base' in Sevastopol and were unsure of their position. They must have feared that they were at risk of being finished off with their prisoners if the different bands, which now and then came to the gates and insisted upon being let in, did actually break in. Therefore they categorically refused admittance to Djulber to anyone who appeared at the gates – and it wasn't always for the best – and wanted to get in. Their cautiousness and fear possibly saved the family from falling victim to the revolutionary terrorists. We realised that this state of things could not last for long and that something had to break the tension.

Countess Zinaide Mengden*: The Roll-Call at Ai-Todor and the Move to Djulber 1917.

On the 19th of February a commission arrived from Sevastopol to find out whether we were all there. It was a strange crowd of different types of people and not exactly confidence-inspiring...

On the 20th of February we heard that there was talk about moving us from Ai-Todor to a neighbouring estate, Djulber, which belonged to Grand Duke Peter, who was the brother of the former generalissimo Nicholas .... Soon it proved to be a fact and we all got busy with the packing, as the move was going to take place on the 26th of February. It was deemed more practical to have us under custody at Djulber because the house was surrounded by a high wall on three sides whilst there was a steep slope straight down to the sea on the fourth side. It would be easier to guard us here.

Source: "The Memoirs of the Countess Zinaide Mengden"*, pages 123–124

CHAPTER 22

A Bitter Farewell

*T**he Commissar in whose district we lived in then was an idealist, and absolutely different to all the other commissars who were in positions of power round about the country. His wish was not to kill – on the contrary he did everything he could to save lives, especially those of women and children. As part of his efforts he had plans to establish a sort of 'self-defence' group to take up the fight against the terrorist bands that roamed round the countryside in huge lorries, and who killed and plundered wherever they appeared. The specific afternoon I am writing about was when the Commissar had summoned some of the male inhabitants to a meeting – among others my husband. They were going to discuss what could be done to protect the place against these attacks. I was at home and just thinking of getting the coffee ready for his return. Suddenly, I heard a terrible noise outside. I ran to the window and just managed to see chickens and a huge lorry, full of shouting and screaming armed men, speed past our little house and disappear in a cloud of dust. Someone called out to me: 'get away as quickly as you can!' Quite bewildered, and not knowing what to do without my husband, I grabbed my baby and jumped out of the low window at the back of the house. There I stood at my wits' end, but luckily I met my husband on the path and together we got out of the way. We disappeared up the mountainside where we assumed that we would be in relative safety. From our hiding place we saw the lorry come back. It was now driving slowly, so we caught a glimpse of our poor Commissar under arrest and being hurried away in the opposite direction. He looked pale and miserable. On our return next morning a young boy came running up to us. He was eager to give us some news and said that the Commissar had been shot a short distance from our house, and that his body had been thrown over a stone wall. Some neighbours had found it and taken it away. That poor man had been too moderate for the terrorist bands.*

We had spent the night with some friends, who lived up in the mountains but returned the following morning. This murder made such an impression on us that we decided not to take any unnecessary risks, and as we did not want to share the same fate as the commissar we disappeared up the mountain again towards evening, knocked at our friends' door and spent the night with them again. It turned out that the lorry's visit to the village had been a final, desperate act of terrorism. The following day all the terrorists disappeared from the area – in the same way as dew fades away in the morning sun. It all happened so quickly that it was difficult to keep up with. *In the early morning we were awakened by voices in the next room. We listened but could not hear what was being said. Then a head popped in and we could hardly believe the news that the prisoners of Djulber were free … at last and that in some extraordinary manner – all the bad elements had disappeared. We quickly got dressed and hurried over to Djulber. It was a day or two before Easter, and I doubt that we ever had a happier Easter than the one we then had with our loved ones after having been separated for such a long time. The Easter message: 'Christ has risen' had never sounded more blissful in our ears than on that day, which brought light and happiness after so many difficult and dark days.*

Later on, we witnessed a sea-battle between two ships. It was a strange sight but we could not see how it ended, as we lost sight of the combatants on the horizon. What could be the reason for this sudden change from death to life? Strange as it may seem it was because of the unexpected arrival of German troops.

During all this period there were many kind people who at different times tried to help my mother get away from Djulber. One of the first ones was Dr. C. Krebs from the Danish Legation in St. Petersburg. His journey to the Crimea turned out to be a whole adventure, and was quite arduous as he had to lie stretched out on his stomach on the roof of the train for part of his journey. The train was very crowded so that was his only chance of getting to the Crimea. Then there was also a Major Boyle, a Canadian, who came on a Romanian ship and had been sent by the Queen of Romania. He tried to persuade Mother to leave with him and get away from the dangers which threatened her. There were still more: one late afternoon a huge Englishman appeared. He was a naval officer by the name of Turle, and didn't look particularly impressive when he arrived as his clothes were at least two sizes too small for him and he was wet through. It turned out that he had been sent off in a small sailing boat to find out if my mother was still alive. The boat had capsized some way from land, but he had managed to swim ashore and had walked miles until he found the house wherein my mother lived. He was tired but in very good spirits and was the first to laugh at his clothes which he had borrowed from a comrade for the trip. They had shrunk so much after having been in the water that he said that he could only get into them with a shoe horn. He asked Mother if there was anything he could help with, but after he found out that she wanted to stay, he left again by boat after darkness had fallen. To all these offers of help to leave the Crimea my mother would say 'no thank-you'. She was grateful for all this kindness and appreciated that there were men who were prepared to risk their lives for her sake, but flatly refused to leave the Crimea. She felt that it was her duty to remain in the country whose Empress she had once been and to which she had given a son and an Emperor.

It was only about a year later that Mother felt that it was time to leave. It was when an English cruiser, the HMS Marlborough, *arrived in the waters close to Djulber and the captain rowed ashore. When he told her that he refused to be responsible for her and the family if they did not come with him, she relented. Via Constantinople and Malta, Mother travelled to England where she stayed for a short while with her sister, Queen Alexandra, and then returned to her beloved Denmark on the merchant ship 'Fiona'.*

This is, however, a part of Mother's life which I cannot describe from personal experience. My husband and I did not join her on the journey. *About three months previously, we had left the Crimea and settled in the Caucasus. It happened like this: for as long as German troops occupied the Crimea there was no danger brewing for Mother and the rest of us. But as they started withdrawing, black ominous clouds had alas again started gathering over the little family clan. Security had been replaced by uncertainty. No one knew what tomorrow would bring. My husband and I talked about the situation, and agreed that it would hardly be wise to stay in the Crimea much longer. I was soon expecting my second baby and was getting nervous that my condition might stop us from leaving. We wanted to go somewhere else while we still had the opportunity to do so, and discussed the matter with Mother and the others again and again. Finally, the air became so tense that we decided to carry out our plans. We packed up our small possessions and waited for the first possible ship to Novorossisk. If we could get there we would still be in our mother country. That part of Russia was then still in the hands of the 'Whites'.*

We had some time to wait as the ships were most irregular like all other means of traffic, and you could never know when a ship would turn up. After literally sitting on our cases for about three weeks a passenger ship suddenly appeared. This was the signal for our departure. It was January 1st, 1919. We rushed over to Mother to say goodbye but were not given a kindly reception. She was very upset and angry that we were leaving, and said that she had never heard a word about us having any plans of the sort. We tried to remind her of our conversations about the subject during the past month and added that we had to think of our children, the one we had and the one we were expecting, but like most elderly people she did not want to be reminded of anything unpleasant and refused to remember anything at all. She was adamant about our responsibility towards her. We stressed the point that we had just as much responsibility towards our children, and their future and that the 'mouse-trap' – as we called the Crimea – was one you had to get away from before it snapped shut round us all … It was a sad and bitter parting but we never regretted what we did. We bade farewell to all our loved ones and set out. Luckily, we found a vacant cabin on board which we and baby Tihon shared with a comrade of my husband's. The voyage did not have a good start. We ran into a thick fog in the Bay of Kertch, and as there was a mine-field nearby, and the captain did not know exactly where it was, we had to anchor there for the whole night and wait till the sun cleared the fog.

The following day we continued to Novorossisk and arrived there safely. In one or the other way the rumour about our arrival must have sped ahead of us because we had only been there for a very short while when General Kutiepov came to see us. Some people will remember that it was this general who disappeared in Paris some years ago under very strange circumstances.

The general made us very welcome and offered us the loan of his private carriage if we wished to continue our journey by train. We were very happy to accept his offer and the following day we travelled on to the small Cossack town of Novominskaya, where we had planned to stay for a while. It was about midnight when we got there. It was a moonlit night and bitterly cold. We were welcomed by a wonderful supper table with both duck, chicken, pies and many other tasty dishes, which we had not had in the Crimea. I was very hungry and for the first and last time in my life I almost ate a whole duck on my own. It was a most delightful change from Crimean food! We had rented a small house, which consisted of four rooms and a kitchen. A large orchard also belonged to the house. It stretched right down to the banks of a river. The place was pretty in winter but when the spring came and the thaw sat in, it was a truly delightful place. We busied ourselves in our vegetable garden, and got much pleasure out of it as the climate was marvellous. In April all the fruit trees were in bloom – there were especially many cherry trees. As you looked down the long village street from our house, you could hardly see the cottages for the white cherry-blossoms on either side. On such a warm sunny day my second boy was born. We called him Guri after Guri Panaev of my regiment. He and his two brothers had, incidentally, lost their lives in the war.

My little Guri was christened three days after I had him. One of the regiment's officers was his godfather. He had quite by chance arrived in the area a few days before, and when he heard that we were staying there he hastened to visit us. He had been wounded twice and had been admitted to our hospital both times, but had survived in one piece. We were very pleased to see him, and that he agreed to act as godfather, because we felt that it was yet another link to the good old days which we still hoped to see again. Unfortunately, we were disappointed in that respect but then on the other hand there were so many other things to be pleased with – especially with our two lovely sons who, with their happy prattling and dear smiles, always managed to make us forget both sorrows and adversity. The four of us had each other.

Countess Zinaide Mengden*: Request to the Danish Legation in Petrograd for help, Letter Prince Schervaschidze 23rd January 1918

We occasionally succeeded in smuggling a letter out of our prison in an empty milk bottle which was brought back to the shop. This is how Prince Schervaschidze got a letter sent off to the Danish ambassador (Scavenius) in Petrograd on the 23rd of January 1918.

Ai-Todor, 23rd January 1918

Dear Mr. Scavenius

I have long wanted to write to you, but it is only today that there is a convenient opportunity to send you a letter, and I hasten to take advantage of it.

This letter will be handed over to you by Mr. N. N., who will be travelling on his own to Petrograd on this mission and who will be staying there for as long as you need time to write an answer, which he will bring back to me here. Since my last letter, which Prince Dolgorouky handed over to you or to be more precise, since 26th October all of us, who are at Ai-Todor, have been completed cut off from the outside world.

We are not permitted to go outside the fence which surrounds Ai-Todor's Park, and we can only receive those people, who are our acquaintances. Newspapers, letters and telegrams only reach us occasionally because the railways hardly function. This is why we know nothing about what is going on in Russia and especially not what is happening in Petrograd. We don't even know whether we are still at war or have made peace with Germany.

But even though the gates to our park are closed to us, then they are unfortunately very much open to reckless gangs, which snoop around, and who do not recognise any sort of authority.

For three days last week we heard the noise of canon shots and mitrailleuse (machine guns); our servants told us that there were two armed political parties who were fighting for power in Yalta, that there were many victims and that some retired officers, who had been living peacefully in the town etc., had been shot and drowned.

Foodstuffs are starting to become really scarce, and it looks like we will be threatened by a veritable famine within a very short time. Furthermore, the banks in Yalta are generally closed, and even when they are open, they refuse to pay out much needed money from our own accounts; we are thus totally without money.

Mr. N. N. has been given instructions to provide you with detailed information about our life here.

Her Majesty, the Empress's two daughters and the rest of us all live at Ai-Todor. We all agree that there is no power in Russia, which would be able to protect Her Majesty from arbitrary demands and acts of violence by the different local, demagogic organisations, which from time to time suddenly come into being, and which replace each other, soon Sevastopol, soon in Yalta, in Koreis and in other places. By continuing to remain at Ai-Todor under the present conditions, Her Majesty would be exposing herself to humiliations and dangers, which will continue to increase. It is consequently necessary to protect her against these calamities by giving her a possibility to leave Ai-Todor and be taken to a place, where Her Majesty would be out of harm's way.

I can only think of two places, which would be suitable for this: Denmark, Her Majesty's beloved mother country, and Finland where she has always been loved by the population. But then there is the big question: When and how could such a plan be carried out? Unfortunately, I am not at all in a position to give you any advice. Grand Duke Alexander Michaelovich, Prince Dolgorouky and I live here like in a prison; we know nothing about what is going on outside Ai-Todor and we see no one; thus we are totally unable to arrange anything and we haven't the slightest idea about how to go about this matter.

But even though it saddens me to find myself in such an embarrassing situation, I am happy to know that in you Her Majesty has an energetic and chivalrous advocate, who is always ready to protect her interests.

In your capacity as Denmark's Minister you are the only person at the moment, whose assistance and support we are able to ask for in our efforts to ease Her Majesty's fate, and it is with hope and confidence that I accept your judgement, your efforts and decision in the question which occupies us here.

The only point, which I am completely sure of is that Her Majesty's journey must be completely official, in other words that Her Majesty be accompanied on the way by a delegate from the Central Government

(People's Commissars) and – if you think this is possible – also by a representative of the Danish Legation.

Incidentally, I can neither give you any instructions or advice. Considering the wretched condition of the railways, I have no idea whether it would be possible for Her Majesty's train to be driven right through the whole of Russia all the way to Finland or whether it would be easier to arrange the journey on a French steamship from here to Constanza (and then continue on to Denmark from there).

I will leave it up to you to make the decision in these important questions. I only ask that you understand that her Majesty would never agree to leave these places without being able to take her daughter, the Grand Duchess Xenia and her family, along with her.

Believe me, dear Mr. Scavenius, this is what I consider my duty to inform you of.

Your noble and courageous attitude last summer under Kerensky's government is a guarantee for me that you will act along the same lines under the present circumstances. I regret that I am so far away from you and am unable to be of help with anything in this matter.

With the greatest impatience I now await the answer, which you consider appropriate to send me by the bearer of this letter.

In anticipation hereof, please accept my kindest regards.

I remain yours respectfully, your devoted G. Schervaschidze.

P.S. Mr. N. N. is a man, who enjoys Grand Duke Alexander Michaelovich's complete confidence. He speaks very good German. During his whole stay in Petrograd he will be at your disposal to give you all the details you will need.

The Danish doctor Krebs was in Russia as a Red Cross delegate and had just returned home from a trip to Siberia when the Prince's letter arrived at the Danish legation in Petrograd... Chamberlain Scavenius immediately asked Dr. Krebs to go to the Crimea to bring the help that was needed and tried to meet Lenin to discuss the matter, but he did not succeed. But Dr. Krebs was all the same able to set out after he had succeeded in exchanging a few words with Trotsky. It was a big and happy surprise for the Empress, when Doctor Krebs finally reached Ai-Todor with quite a supply of foodstuffs and money

... 21st April: In the evening we had an Easter service together with some visiting neighbours. Later, we had the Easter meal over at Grand Duke Nicholas' place... .... After consulting with Grand Duke Nicholas and Grand Duchess Xenia, the Empress decided to move to Harax. This estate belonged to Grand Duke George Michaelovich, who was married to Princess Marie of Hellenes .... Grand Duke Alexander and Grand Duchess Xenia wanted to go back to Ai-Todor with their children. On the 26th of May there was a farewell luncheon at Grand Duke Nicholas' after which we separated. The Empress then moved to Harax with Prince Dolgoruky and me, the two Cossack life guards and the whole of the female staff ... When we were told that the Bolsheviks had already reached the Crimea and could be expected in Yalta in the course of a few hours, the Empress and Grand Duke Nicholas finally saw themselves forced to give in. But Her Majesty only agreed to leave under the condition that anyone else, who could possibly be exposed to persecution by the Bolsheviks, would be permitted to come too. Prince Dolgoruky requested my brother to initiate relevant negotiations with the English....

...Grand Duke Nicholas arranged for all conditions to be established. March 25th was a busy day. Everyone packed and at the last luncheon at Harax we were gathered to bid farewell to the people who lived at Ai-Todor. At five o'clock in the afternoon the Empress went with her daughter Xenia to Djulber where they said goodbye to their friends and acquaintances, who had gathered on the little jetty. My nephew stood here and kept guard for the last time as a White officer ...

Source: "The Memoirs of the Countess Zinaide Mengden"*, pages 125–128, 137, 149

Prince Roman Romanoff: – Empress Marie Feodorovna's Departure from the Crimea 1919.

On the 25th March, on the day of the Annunciation of the Virgin Mary, the H.M.S. Marlborough passed Djulber on her way to Yalta. The battle ship was accompanied by two English torpedo boats and was followed by many troopships and smaller vessels, which were going to take refugees on board in Yalta. After loading our luggage the enormous grey battleship Marlborough anchored off Djulber accompanied by a torpedo boat. She lay at some distance from the shore, while the torpedo boat approached the beach to sound out the depth of the water At Djulber everyone was nearly ready to walk down to the jetty at Koriez, where the English had told us to gather ...

I quickly ran down the hill and reached the jetty. Apart from my parents and sisters, who were waiting in the group of passengers, there was also my paternal uncle Nikolasha, my maternal aunt Stana, the families Tyszkewicz, Yussupov. Dolgoruky, Countess Olga Orlova, members of the entourage and servants with quite a bit of baggage. Nicholas Orlov and Pavel Fersen were already on board the Marlborough where the Commander had asked them to help receive the passengers and allocate cabins to them. Right at the end of the long jetty, which had been built on poles, stood a group of English sailors and an officer and a sloop lay at the mooring post.

Shortly after, the Dowager Empress arrived with Aunt Xenia and her sons. The Dowager Empress was dressed in a black coat and wore a small black hat on her head. She walked in silence past us towards the jetty. She was followed by Aunt Xenia and her sons, who had arrived in another car. When the Dowager Empress reached the end of the jetty, she walked down into the sloop with the English military flag, while the sailors saluted. As soon as Aunt Xenia was on board with the "Alexandrovichs", the sloop set sail and headed for the Marlborough.

Another sloop immediately approached the jetty. It took Uncle Nikolasha, Aunt Stana, my parents, my sisters and me on board and we immediately put off from the shore ...

Source: "The Memoirs of Roman Romanoff, Prince of Russia, 1896–1919"
Pages 498–499

CHAPTER 23

With the Kuban Cossacks

*T*wo weeks after Guri's birth my husband and I started to join in the every-day work in the area. Together with the other villagers, and our two babies, we would set out to the fields in the early morning and hoe till late in the afternoon. Most of the time baby Guri would sleep peacefully in an old manger which we had filled with straw. Tihon, who was not quite two years old, would run around our legs and hinder us immensely in our work. We had to keep a con-stant eye on him as we didn't want him to get hurt.

Field work was naturally hard and unaccustomed for both of us, but none the less I felt so happy at this time. It was just the right kind of life we were leading. We worked for our daily bread, we were young and healthy and we had two lovely babies to look after and enjoy. I could not have wished for a better life. We had found a refuge again and felt far away from turmoil and misery. We even had faint hopes of being able to lead this peaceful life until things righted themselves and life became normal again. Alas – that was not to be. We naturally encountered many problems which had never come our way before. There was, for example, such a minor thing as drinking water. There was a river close to our house but its water was not safe to drink. Fortunately, we had a well in the yard and when it couldn't supply us with sufficient water we managed with rainwater, and the dew which dripped down from the roof into a special container. That was the way it was done here and we quickly accustomed ourselves to it. On the whole, there was a lot which was different to what I had been used to. Even if it was a matter of nature it was different to what I had known earlier. Here were no woods and no spring flowers – how I longed for them – but only one unending steppe after the other for miles and miles. Wherever you looked you would stare out over never-ending fields. However, they had their beauty and poetry too. The larks would sing so beau-tifully, and numerous green and brown lizards would dart about between the tufts of grass or lie in the hot sunshine by the roadside.

It didn't take long before we made new friends. We were especially attached to a doctor and his family who lived and worked in the village. He was 29 and she 27. They were an extremely likeable couple. He would lend me books to read and was happy to come and chat with us. They had a little boy of a year and a half who they always brought with them. He and Tihon became friends and playmates.

It was unfortunate that after a while the doctor's visits became more and more seldom. A malignant typhus fever had broken out in the area, and our loveable doctor was kept busy from early morning till far into the night. At one period there were between ten and eleven deaths every day in our little town. Our poor young doctor had so much work heaped upon his shoulders that we hardly ever saw him. He was seldom at home and barely had time to eat or even sleep.

Time and again we would see him being taken from house to house, with seven or eight carts following to take him in turn to the other sick homes. The young doctor grew thinner and thinner and looked really dreadful. The last time we saw him he said: 'My life cannot last long; I am tired out and know that now my turn will soon come.' We tried to console him and cheer him up as best as we could, but I could see by his eyes that he was not convinced of his chances. He was right. About a week after my Guri's birth, he caught typhus fever and died within a few days. The enormous crowd that came to his funeral showed how much he had been loved and appreciated. Thus ended a life which had been so full of promise. He had not only studied and become a doctor in his own country, but had also taken the time to study in Paris and spoke French like a Frenchman. His poor young widow, who was a doctor and surgeon too, first tried to take over his work, but she did not have the strength to stay on where everything reminded her of her terrible loss. She found a place in a hospital in a town somewhere else and left with her young son. I never heard from her since but have often wondered whether she ever came to terms with her fate. Those two people loved each other so much.

Before leaving, the doctor's wife had given me her baby's old pram. It was made of wicker and the handle was missing, but I was happy to have it since prams were an unknown luxury in those parts. One afternoon, I was sitting on a seat outside the house by the road enjoying the lovely sunny weather. I had put Guri in the 'basket' on wheels, and he was fast asleep. A woman passed by and glanced curiously at it. Then she stopped and asked me: 'What have you got to sell in your basket?' I answered that it was only my son and that he was not for sale. She walked away slightly disappointed.

The summer was beautiful that year, and many old friends visited and stayed with us. We didn't have much room so they slept in a narrow glass veranda which was a nice place during the summer.

We quickly made good friends with our neighbours and helped each other as one does in the country. It didn't take long before the word went round that I had once been a nurse, and the villagers would come to me with cuts and burns or arm or leg injuries. We were really quite adept at curing their minor injuries. In return and as a thank-you they would often bring us a chicken, a duck or a cart-load full of delicious watermelons. Our garden gave us so much fruit – both cherries and particularly apricots. During the time the apricots were ripe we had so many that we couldn't eat them all up – even though we had the chickens to help! Our stay in this small, quiet village was a perfect idyll. Every morning it was amusing to see how the peasants let their cows out into the road, where a young shepherd lad would drive the whole herd – about 300 – out to the steppe. In the evening he would drive them home again – and each single cow knew its own gate and would trot slowly into its stable. It was a highly amusing sight.

There was a young peasant woman in the village by the name of Maryushka, who used to come over to help me with the heavier housework. She was good at using her hands and a dear soul, but she always looked dreadfully sad. I was awfully sorry for her because her husband, a soldier, had disappeared and for over a year she had had no news of him. Maryushka was very superstitious and would run from one fortune-teller to the other to find out about him. She always had the same question: 'Where is my husband? Is he dead or alive?' They all answered that he was alive, but he never returned – at any rate not for as long as we were down there. Apparently, it did not shake her belief that she would one day have him back again. One day, she came over to me with a big, round loaf of newly baked bread. It was still hot out of the oven. She ran into the living room, where I was sitting and said: 'Now you can think of someone you would like to hear about – if he is alive then the bread will turn!' We held the loaf between us – using but two fingers each. By its mere weight the soft warm bread sunk down on our uplifted fingers. We waited – I thought of someone – and to my incredible surprise the loaf began to move slowly and then it turned round and round all by itself. Maryushka looked at me triumphantly and said: "Can you see? – the person you are thinking of is alive!"

Some time later I had a strange experience. I had a little white poodle that was called 'Lock'. One day he ran away. I was very upset because Lock was such a dear little fellow. We searched everywhere for him but could not find him, and there was no one who had seen or heard anything of him. Two nights after he had disappeared, my husband and I woke up by our bed being shaken and the sound of claws on the bare floor. That made us very happy since we thought it must be Lock who had come home. I called him but he didn't come. It was strange because our bed was still being pushed about, and the sound of feet and claws continued. We lay there a bit and thought that he was sure to come, but since he still did not show up we got up and struck a match. There was no sign of Lock. Then we lit a candle and looked under the bed and round the empty room – there was nothing.

After we had made a thorough search we went back to bed but directly we blew out the light – it all began again. The bed was given one push after the other and the mysterious scratching started all over again. We could not solve the riddle – and much mystified we went to sleep! When Maryushka arrived the next morning to wash the floor, I told her about the night's strange happening. She looked at me with a pair of huge, black eyes and said in a subdued tone: 'That is a sure sign that you will soon leave this house – it is the house-ghost who is sending you away!' Of course, we laughed at her but she just shook her superstitious head uneasily and said: 'Yes, just you laugh but you will see that I am right. You will soon be leaving!' And Maryushka and her house-ghost were right. Shortly after, my husband and I decided to leave. It is really difficult for me to explain what it was that made us leave this lovely spot but when you live a primitive life in a time of danger, like we did with the Kuban Cossacks, one gets a strong feeling of intuition – more instinct than reason. In the autumn both my husband and I instinctively felt that the time had come to leave.

We packed up our meagre belongings and told Maryushka that we would be off. She was so sad and emotional that she couldn't even manage to say the customary: 'I told you so. What did I say? The household spirit always gets its way!' She just cried and cried – and I couldn't help shedding a tear either because I had been so happy in these peaceful surroundings.

CHAPTER 24

Yet Another Flight

*I*t had been our intention to travel to a town in the north, but to get there we
would have to pass through Rostov. On the way both my husband and I had
an uncanny feeling that it was wrong of us to travel northwards, and we talked
about it at some length. Just as we were sitting discussing all the reasons there
could be for not travelling north, an officer walked into our compartment. We did
not know him but when we got talking and told him about our plans, he told us
in so many words that it would be sheer madness to go to the town where we had
originally thought of settling. He advised us most definitely to stay in Rostov for
the time being, and we considered it to be a sign from above. My husband and I
were both most surprised, but at the same time very happy, to have such a quick
and final solution to our doubts. Now the decision had been made: we were going
to stay in Rostov – and we felt very happy and relieved. Our unknown friend was
even kind enough to arrange for lodgings for us with a rich widow who lived in
Rostov and there we stayed for a week as her guests, but since we did not want to
take advantage of her kindness we looked for somewhere else where we could stay.
After a week we found a suitable place. It was an Armenian monastery which lay
some twenty kilometres outside the town of Rostov. In reality, it was only the
remains of a monastery we came to, as the place had apparently once been stormed
and badly damaged. The doors which hadn't already been reduced to matchwood,
were swinging helplessly on the leftovers of their hinges. Most of the windows had
been smashed and the furniture had received the same treatment. The monastery
was situated on a cliff surrounded by summer villas and parks, and if they had
been in order and it had been summer it would undoubtedly have been a most
pleasant place to stay. Now it was deserted and dismal. We chose to settle in a long
white wing where there were four rooms, and we did what we could to make it
as comfortable as we possibly could with the available means. We filled some sacks
with hay and stuck them in the places where the window glass was missing, and
found some doors which were more or less useable. To our immense surprise and
extreme relief, we discovered that the stove could heat all four rooms nicely. There
was enough kindling wood in the surroundings – and with that the difficult heating
problem was safely over and done with.

We arrived at the monastery in the autumn and assumed that we would, at *any rate, be spending the winter here. Our stay did, however, turn out to be considerably shorter, and we only spent three and a half months there. At first, before the cold and snow set in, we would go for walks in the neighbourhood. We would even sometimes venture inside one of the neighbouring villas that had been wrecked and looted by the marauders, and were always half afraid of what could meet our eyes. In the nicest houses we came across furniture that had been smashed, paintings that had been slashed or cut out of their frames; and it wasn't difficult to imagine what had been going on when we noticed how the floors were littered with broken glass and empty wine bottles. In many places the marauders had pulled up the floor boards to search for hidden treasures which the owners had possibly wanted to hide. There was dreadful destruction everywhere we went. It was not a reassuring sight. In many places things had taken place which cannot be put into print. All the villas in the area had been abandoned. You could see that from their overgrown gardens which were rich with wild vine. Their big red leaves hung like huge drops of blood in garlands and festoons from balconies and trees, and made you think of death and destruction further emphasizing the sinister atmosphere.*

Very seldom, but still now and then, friends from Rostov would come out to visit us. They always had to hurry back to town before dark as so many robberies and murders were the order of the day after nightfall. Even though we did not own anything that could even tempt the poorest robber, we lived in constant fear that one of the vagrant robber bands would find its way to us. One day, there was a sudden knock at our door which so rarely happened. Outside stood a wretched, poor woman. She had been attacked and beaten and was bleeding from many sores. The robbers who had stopped her had taken her money, her pitiful coat and her boots. She stood there bare-footed and in nothing but her thin dress. She had been to the market in Rostov with some goods, and on the way home with her meagre earnings she had been robbed some way from our monastery. Somehow, she had managed to drag herself up to our door. What a poor soul she was!

A way into December we again had the feeling that it would soon be time to leave the monastery. One early morning we received the news that we should leave that same afternoon as Rostov was being evacuated. We were prepared for this and had already packed up our bundles, ready to leave at a minute's warning. All we now had to do was to roll up our babies in warm shawls and get into the sledge which we had ready. My husband got into the driver's seat with his gun slung across his wide shoulders. I sat behind with the children, and then we were off. We drove and drove. Suddenly there was a bump in the uneven road, and the gun slipped off my husband's shoulder and knocked against poor Tihon's little nose.

You can still see the scar. It was a frosty but calm evening. There was snow every-where you looked, the sun was setting and lit up the whole of the snowy steppe with its last rays. The closer we got to Rostov, the big town which was our desti-nation, the more people there were on the roads hurrying towards it like we were. Some came on foot and carried their bundles on their backs. Others were driving cattle along, and dragging their possessions along on a small sledge. Somewhere else we met a man riding a fine horse, and who was trying to manage a string of racing horses which he wanted to rescue from the danger zone. People brought the strangest things along with them. It was evident that all they could think of was to save what they cherished most, and that without the slightest thought of having any chance of taking it with them and whether it could be of any use to them in the future.

The sun was about to disappear on the horizon when we arrived in Rostov. From there we hoped to continue our journey by train. Here conditions were even more confusing and chaotic than on the country roads, and it was dusk before we reached the station. On the way we met tram-cars filled with casualties who were being moved by train from their hospitals to a town some distance away. The station itself was seething with activity. Everyone was asking questions but no one could answer them. We managed to get into a train carriage but hadn't a notion of when it would leave and where it would be going. Many people begged to be taken in too. In our compartment there were three officers and one of them had his young wife with him. All three officers were suffering from typhoid fever. They were so weak that they had to lie on the floor as there was no room for them anywhere else.

We were happy to have found seats in the train and were just waiting for it to drive off. However, it seemed that no one was interested in our train. We watched one overfilled train after the other drive off on the other tracks. Several times we thought of getting out of our train which had apparently been forgotten by its staff, and try to corner a seat in one of the other trains, but we dared not run the risk. If we had just left our seats for a second, they would immediately have been taken over by others. After our train had stood still on a siding for two days and two nights we noticed that someone suddenly started showing interest in us, and just as we had given up all hope of continuing our journey, the train slowly pulled out of the station.

My brain was in quite a daze after all the waiting and unbearable suspense of not knowing whether we would manage to leave before 'anything happened'. However, as soon as we felt the train moving, we calmed down – and then we dis-covered that it was Christmas Eve! One of the ill officers got out at a station to buy a sausage and some bread, which he shared with us by the light of a candle stump. That was a strange Christmas Eve – so unlike the happy ones of my child-hood. Now we were travelling with three terminally ill people in a pitch-dark carriage without the slightest idea of where we were going. We missed everything that normally belongs to a proper Christmas, right from the church service to the Christmas fare and the presents, but all the same we were happy and fortunate because we had saved our lives and we had each other.

In due time our train stopped at a small station. We got off as we knew that there was a small Cossack town nearby where we would be given a warm welcome, and that proved correct. There we were given lodgings, and fed and treated very kindly for two weeks. An old grandmother lived in the cottage we had stayed in. She would sit at her spinning wheel repeating one psalm after the other. She could not read or write, yet from early childhood she had been taught the New Testament and the psalms and knew both by heart. She was rich in this learning as were so many of her generation, and was respected by her sons and grandchildren. All Cossack towns are kept extremely clean, and virtually once a month the houses are scrubbed and white-washed thoroughly both inside and out so that they simply shine with cleanliness. We quickly got to know many of the villagers, and they invited us to visit them one evening after the other. There were many who asked us whether we wouldn't want to settle down in the region and buy a piece of land. The idea appealed to us and we even looked at some very nice places for sale, but we did not dare believe that we would be able to live in peace and that thought made us so nervous that we decided to travel on after a few weeks. We were reluctant to do so, but we were uneasy about staying. All our new kind friends and their families – in other words all the villagers – accompanied us to the train and we were given so many provisions that they lasted us for weeks. We hung out of the windows for as long as we could see the last furry Cossack cap – we had been so happy there.

So we were off again, and this time bound for the Black Sea port of Novorossisk. It was a horrible journey. Our wagon was dirty and full of bugs that left us alone during the daytime, but fed on us at nightfall. I remember sitting up with a candle stump and crushing the horrid things, as they marched in procession out of cracks and corners to attack my poor sleeping children, but nothing could stop them. There were too many of them, and they were too crafty and too greedy for me to put a damper on their appetite.

From the flat country of the steppes, we arrived one evening at a mountain station from where the steep descent starts towards the Black Sea through numerous tunnels, which is why the station had been given the name 'Tunelnaja'. Shortly before we were due to leave, I was standing at one of the cracked windows in the corridor and there I overheard a conversation between two railway officials, which made my blood run cold. One of them said: 'Did you say that there are only three brakes?' – 'Yes, only three and there are ninety-three wagons'. – 'Do you think that they can hold the train?' – 'No, they most certainly can't.' – 'Yes, but ... what can we do?' – 'Well, we could try something else – the only thing I can suggest is that we add on an empty petroleum cistern that has a brake – that might help!!! I told my husband about the conversation, and even though neither of us was anxious by nature, we lay awake for most of the night listening to how the four brakes screeched and shrieked while trying to save our lives. It was no fun to race down a hill through one tunnel after the other knowing that our lives hung – not on a thread, but on four delicate iron clenches.

CHAPTER 25

Home to Denmark

*W*ell, *I hope I shall never have to travel again in a ninety-three wagon-long train with only four brakes, and travel downhill for a whole long night all through tunnels in pitch darkness ... by God's mercy we arrived safely at the Black Sea the following morning, which was very black-looking that January winter day.*

The town didn't look at all inviting. It was packed with refugees and it was impossible to find lodgings anywhere. There was nothing to be done but to stay in our train in the company of the intolerable bugs. It was fortunate that an old friend – a Cossack officer, whom we knew from St. Petersburg – found us there later in the day. He was now quartermaster in Novorossisk, and before he left he promised to do his best to find somewhere in town where we could stay.

He kept his word. That same afternoon he returned with a kind-looking giant following him. He was the Danish Consul, Thomas Schytte, who invited us to stay in his home – an offer we naturally accepted with enthusiasm. We were only too happy to escape from the dirt and the bugs, to even try to make a secret out of our delight at his invitation.

We stayed with the Consul for the next month; he was awfully dear and kind to us. During that time we had ample opportunity to see how he went out of his way to help his countrymen as much as he could, when they were in need of a helping hand. He gave them food if they were hungry, provided them with clothes if they were cold, and arranged for tickets for them if they wanted to go home and so on. One day, the Consul said to us: 'Of course, you want to go to Denmark, don't you? Everybody wants to go there!' He himself was naturally longing to get home to his wife and children, but even when we left he was obliged to stay on to do his work to the end. He was definitely not the type of person who would run away from his responsibilities.

We sailed from Novorossisk on board the passenger ship 'Habsburg', which was dreadfully overcrowded. Shortly before we were due to set sail, one of our acquaintances, a general, asked if we wouldn't prefer to travel on a small yacht, where his son served as an officer. He promised us that we would be very comfortable and sincerely advised us to accept his offer. We gave the idea some thought as it naturally sounded tempting, but then our subconsciousness again warned us not to accept his friendly offer. We knew that we had made the right decision when we heard that the yacht had struck a rock not far from Varna, on the Bulgarian coast. There wasn't much room on the 'Habsburg' but we managed all the same. We had grown accustomed to living under primitive conditions. Every day at a certain hour, all the mothers with young children would be allowed into the ship's kitchen, so that they could prepare the food themselves that they wanted to give their children. We naturally met many people on board who we knew, so there was plenty of opportunity to ask for news from all parts. Unfortunately, most of it was sad.

After a rather rough passage we reached the Dardanelles. Here, the ship had to stop because of quarantine, and those passengers who wished to go to Constantinople had to leave the ship. They got off and were taken ashore in an open boat. The rest of us were towed to the small island of Tuzla, not far from the Asiatic coast, where we were going to be disinfected. We were taken ashore and spent all that day in the open air. Thank God it was warm and sunny that day.

In parties of ten or twelve – the men on one side, the women on the other – we were ordered into cold wooden sheds where we had to strip and stand under hot showers while all our clothes were taken away to be fumigated. That took quite a time, and we felt the cold terribly while we were waiting for our clothes. When we finally got them back, they were dripping wet from the steam in the cauldrons. It had been worst for the poor women who had been rash enough to leave their gloves or leather belts among their clothes. They got them back as small stiff, shrunken lumps which could not be used for anything at all. One poor soul lost her shoes in this manner. When she got them back, they were crumpled, useless and the size of a pair of children's shoes. Happily, the babies under three were spared the ordeal and spent the time playing outside in the sunshine.

Our toilet completed, we were ordered out again to make room for the next group, and there we sat on our island till sunset. All we were given to drink and eat was a mug of hot black tea and a handful of 'soldiers' biscuits', which kind Hindu soldiers brought us. These slender, tall, handsome men were so picturesque in their white turbans, with their black eyes and dazzling white teeth and they all had a kind smile for the young children. When the sun was about to set, it was all over and we were sent back to the ship in a big open barge which was towed to the island of Prinkipo. Night had fallen by the time we got there, and after the sun had set it was cold and damp on the Bosporus. Under these circumstances it was a miracle that none of us caught pneumonia or malaria on the way.

The island was a lovely place. It was highest in the middle and from there you had a most beautiful view of pine woods, parks, gardens and lots of beautiful villas which were almost like small palaces. It was here that the rich people of Constantinople used to spend the hot summer months, but we saw nothing of all the luxuries while we were staying there. There was so little room where we stayed that we were eleven adults and two children in three rooms. We were quarantined for almost a fortnight on this 'luxury island', and met a number of friends and acquaintances. We all had sad news for each other and heard many a story of woe, misery, sorrow and ill-fate. We heard how many of our friends and acquaintances had lost their lives during these recent terrible months, about women who had lost their husbands, about mothers who had seen their sons for the last time and about people who had saved their lives but had lost their beloved mother country.

During our two weeks on Prinkipo, we visited Constantinople two or three times. There we could not stop stuffing ourselves with sweet things and cakes, and walked along the Pera, the main street, losing ourselves in wonder at the sight of so much in the shops which we had totally forgotten that you could buy if you had the money. We saw the inside of the beautiful Hagia Sophia that had been built as a Christian church in the Byzantine period, but was now used by the Mohammedans. Before we could go in we were asked to put on slippers as is the custom. The building made a mighty impression on us. There is a legend about a Christian priest from the time when the Turks stormed and conquered the city. He was celebrating mass and was holding the Holy chalice in his uplifted hands. It was then that the Turkish soldiers stormed into the church and up towards the altar to kill him. At that instant the metre-thick wall behind the priest opened up, he walked into it and it closed again saving both him and the holy chalice. Many believe that whenever this church will once again become Christian, the priest will step out of the wall and finish the mass he had begun so many centuries ago. It is, of course, just a legend but we had an experience that made a strong impression on us. After the Sophia Church had become a mosque its walls and ceilings were painted – and most likely several times. All the same, it is astonishing that the angels and paintings of Byzantine saints can still be seen through the 'Mohammedan' paint.

From Constantinople we travelled through Bulgaria to Serbia. Bulgaria was a dismal and rocky country – at least what we saw of it from the train. I remembered all the pictures I had seen in my childhood, and all the stories about Bulgaria and its battles for freedom and independence that I had heard from our servants after they returned from the Turkish war. In Belgrade we spent two weeks as guests of King Alexander. I had known him as a boy but hadn't seen him since he had attended school in St. Petersburg. Now he was grown up and had become a handsome, gifted and friendly man. Belgrade had been badly damaged during the World War, but it was all the same strangely picturesque. We were, of course, fortunate to arrive there in the spring, when the Danube was very full and wide.

The town reminded me of Kiev – but just on a smaller scale. Once we went on an excursion into the woods. They were full of primroses and blue scillas – a lovely sight.

One day during our stay in Belgrade there was a knock at our door, and in walked our friend Consul Schytte. He couldn't stay any longer at Novorossisk and was on his way home to Denmark. We continued our journey together. The beginning of the journey was quite dramatic. I remember one high mountain valley which our train had to cross. The bridge had not yet been rebuilt after the war, and therefore we had to go over an awful-looking wooden construction. The engine pushed the carriages onto it without joining them. We slowly rolled over the wooden construction, and were then 'hauled ashore' by another engine which stood on the opposite side.

I stood at the window during the 'crossing' holding Guri – not yet a year old – in my arms – with my heart throbbing at the sight of the deep gorge and the mountain torrent. The cows grazing down there looked like tiny toys. I wondered if the construction could hold out. Suddenly, my baby started to cry and pressed his little face against my shoulder. He must have instinctively felt the danger.

We arrived in Vienna one evening and were told at the station that we were to go to Aunt Thyra's house, 'Penzing Haus'. It had been opened to receive us, and there we were to spend the night. We had not expected her to be there, but when we drove up under the porch – to my great surprise – there stood my Aunt Thyra (Mama's youngest sister) with her youngest daughter Olga to bid us welcome. I think that they had heard of our arrival through the Danish Legation, and had travelled all day from Gmunden to open up their house to receive us. It goes without saying that we had a lot to tell each other after so many years' separation. When we sat down to supper we noticed that they had no bread or butter and very little to eat, whereas we still had a big loaf of bread, butter and cheese brought from Serbia. We gave them much pleasure by producing it all out of our cases and treating them with all these delicacies. It was a memorable meal! Next day we lunched at a restaurant, and it was well that we had our own bread with us as the meal was more than modest. I saw afterwards, with astonishment, how Aunt Thyra and Olga carefully picked up all the tiny bits of bread that remained near our plates and packed them in a piece of paper to take home.

It had been so nice to see my aunt and cousin again, but we had to leave them all the same and travel on to Denmark, where we arrived one evening. At the time we left the Crimea, Tihon was just over a year old. When I arrived in Copenhagen, I was carrying the sleeping Guri in my arms and when Mother saw him she thought it was Tihon. The scales did not fall from her eyes till my husband turned up shortly after holding the hand of our first-born. He was now two and a half, and had grown quite a bit in the meantime. Mother was so anxious to hear how we were because it was a long time since she had last received a letter. All my recent letters arrived a week after we arrived in our new homeland. We had not seen each other for a little over a year.

And now I am going to put a full stop to my memoirs because our time in little, blessed Denmark belongs to the present and our private lives. It is, however, my wish to say that my husband, my two boys and I are most grateful for the reception we have been given in Mother's homeland.

Grand Duchess Olga Alexandrovna and Colonel Nicholas Kulikovsky with their children, Tihon and Guri, 1920.

Acknowledgements

Throughout the course of writing this book, a number of people in different countries provided inspiration and helped shape the contents of the book. We would like to thank them all very much for their valuable support.

Denmark	Prince Dimitri Romanov, Jørgen Bjerregaard†, Bjarne Steen Jensen, Mette Jensen, Ove Mogensen
Greece	Ian Vorres
Russia	Ludmila Antonova Kulikovsky, Dr. Zinaida I. Peregudowa, Vadim V. Znamenov
Switzerland	Lena Venezia
Ukraine	Elena Postrikova, Marina Zemljanitschenko
United Kingdom	Frances Dimond, Coryne Hall, Ian Shapiro (Argyll Etkin Limited, London), Katrina Warne, Marion and Peter Wynn, Charlotte Zeepvat
United States of America	Prince David Chavchavadze, Arthur Collingworth, Dr. William Lee, Thomas Mansfield

Paul Kulikovsky
Karen Roth-Nicholls
Sue Woolmans

Grand Duchess Olga's Close

Christian IX, King of Denmark
1818–1906

~ Louise, Queen of Denmark
1817–1898

Frederik VIII, King of Denmark
1843–1912

~ Lovisa, Queen of Denmark
1851–1926

Alexandra, Queen of England
1844–1925

~ Edward VII, King of England
1841–1910

George I, King of the Hellenes
1845–1913

~ Olga, Queen of the Hellenes,
1851–1926

**Marie Feodorovna, Empress of
Russia, 1847–1928**

Thyra, Duchess of Cumberland
1853–1933

~ Ernst August, Duke of Cumberland
1845–1923

Valdemar, Prince of Denmark
1858–1939

~ Marie, Princess of Denmark
1865–1909

Christian X, King of Denmark
1843–1912

~ Alexandrine, Queen of Denmark
1851–1926

Aage, Count of Rosenborg
1887–1940

Axel, Prince of Denmark
1888–1964

Erik, Count of Rosenborg
1890–1950

Viggo, Count of Rosenborg
1893–1970

Margrethe, Princess of Denmark
1895–1992

Alexander II, Emperor of Russia
1818–1881

~ Maria Alexandrovna,
Empress of Russia
1824–1880

Nicholas, Grand Duke, Tsarevich of
Russia, 1843–1865

**Alexander III, Emperor of Russia
1845–1894**

Vladimir, Grand Duke of Russia
1847–1909

~ Maria Pavlovna, Grand Duchess of
Russia, 1854–1920

Alexis, Grand Duke of Russia
1850–1908

Maria Alexandrovna, Grand Duchess
of Russia, 1853–1920

~ Alfred, Duke of Sachsen-Coburg
and Gotha, 1844–1900

Serge, Grand Duke of Russia
1857–1905

~ Elisabeth, Grand Duchess of Russia
1864–1918

Paul, Grand Duke of Russia
1860–1919

~ Alexandra, Grand Duchess of
Russia, 1870–1891

Nicholas II, Emperor of Russia
1868–1918

~ Alexandra (Alix), Empress of
Russia, 1872–1918

George, Grand Duke of Russia
1871–1899

Xenia, Grand Duchess of Russia
1875–1960

~ Alexander (Sandro), Grand Duke
of Russia, 1866–1933

Michael, Grand Duke of Russia
1878–1918

~ Natalia Brassova 1880–1952

**Olga, Grand Duchess of Russia
1882–1960**

~ Nicholas Kulikovsky
1881–1958

elations and Descendants

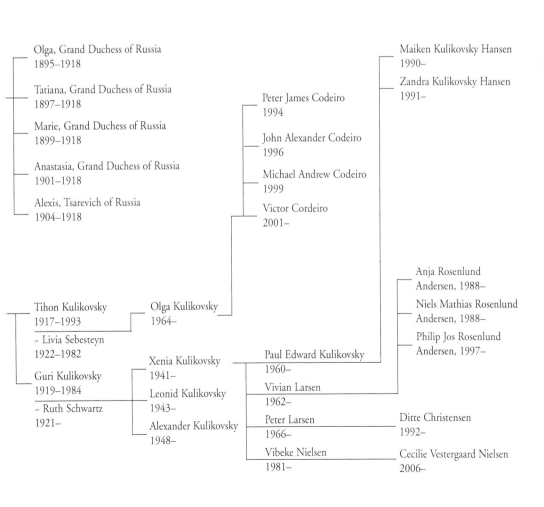

Olga, Grand Duchess of Russia
1895–1918

Tatiana, Grand Duchess of Russia
1897–1918

Marie, Grand Duchess of Russia
1899–1918

Anastasia, Grand Duchess of Russia
1901–1918

Alexis, Tsarevich of Russia
1904–1918

Peter James Codeiro
1994

John Alexander Codeiro
1996

Michael Andrew Codeiro
1999

Victor Cordeiro
2001–

Maiken Kulikovsky Hansen
1990–

Zandra Kulikovsky Hansen
1991–

Tihon Kulikovsky
1917–1993

- Livia Sebesteyn
1922–1982

Guri Kulikovsky
1919–1984

- Ruth Schwartz
1921–

Olga Kulikovsky
1964–

Xenia Kulikovsky
1941–

Leonid Kulikovsky
1943–

Alexander Kulikovsky
1948–

Paul Edward Kulikovsky
1960–

Vivian Larsen
1962–

Peter Larsen
1966–

Vibeke Nielsen
1981–

Anja Rosenlund
Andersen, 1988–

Niels Mathias Rosenlund
Andersen, 1988–

Philip Jos Rosenlund
Andersen, 1997–

Ditte Christensen
1992–

Cecilie Vestergaard Nielsen
2006–

List of Illustrations

Xenia Alexandrovna of Russia, Prince Albert Victor of Wales, Crown Prince Constantine of the Hellenes, Princess Victoria of Wales, Tsarevich Nicholas Alexandrovich of Russia, Princess Alexandra of the Hellenes.

Seated in front: Princess Thyra of Denmark (daughter of Crown Prince Frederick), Edward, Prince of Wales (later King Edward VII), Alexandra, Princess of Wales (later Queen Alexandra), Grand Duchess Olga Alexandrovna of Russia, Empress Marie Feodorovna of Russia, Grand Duke Michael Alexandrovich of Russia, Queen Louise of Denmark, Emperor Alexander III of Russia.

Page 17 Christian IX of Denmark's children 1892. The picture was taken on the occasion of their parents' golden wedding anniversary on May 26th. From left to right: Wilhelm (King George I of the Hellenes), Dagmar (Empress Marie Feodorovna of Russia), Alexandra (Princess of Wales), Frederick (Crown Prince of Denmark), Thyra (Duchess of Cumberland), Valdemar (Prince of Denmark).

Page 19 A family reunion in Fredensborg in 1903 presumably on the occasion of the 40th anniversary of Christian IX's accession to the throne:

(Prince Gustav of Denmark, Princess Dagmar of Denmark, Crown Princess Lovisa of Denmark – hidden).

Back row: Princess Louise of Schaumburg-Lippe, Crown Prince Frederick of Denmark, Queen Alexandra of England, King George I of the Hellenes, King Christian IX of Denmark, Princess Thyra of Denmark, Dowager Empress Marie Feodorovna of Russia, Prince Hans of Glucksburg, Grand Duchess Olga Alexandrovna of Russia, Prince Peter of Oldenburg, Empress Alexandra Feodorovna of Russia, Prince Nicholas of the Hellenes, Princess Victoria of Wales, Grand Duke Michael Alexandrovich of Russia (behind Emperor Nicholas II of Russia), Prince Harold of Denmark, King Edward VII of England, Princess Maud of Wales, (Prince Carl of Denmark, Princess Alexandrine of Denmark – hidden).

In front: Prince Christian & Princess Marie Louise of Schaumburg-Lippe, Grand Duchesses Tatiana, Olga and Marie Nicholaievna of Russia.

CHAPTER 11

CHAPTER 14

CHAPTER 15

CHAPTER 16

Overview

The Extraordinary Life of Olga Alexandrovna – The Last Grand Duchess of Russia

Emperor Alexander III and family 1890.

Grand Duchess Olga Alexandrovna was born in the Cottage Palace in Peterhof, Russia, at 7.30 a.m. on June 1st / 14th, 1882. She was the daughter of Alexander III, Emperor of All the Russias, and his wife, the Empress Marie Feodorovna; and the youngest sister of the next and last Russian Emperor Nicholas II.

Olga was born to unimaginable wealth and splendour. Her life was set against the backdrop of a century. She lived in Russia from her birth till 1920 and was raised under strict and modest circumstances by her parents, governesses and tutors. From a very young age Olga eagerly absorbed everything she saw around her, be it in the palaces in the environs of St. Petersburg or her travels further afield and abroad. She sketched and painted what caught her eye. To foster the natural artistic talent young Olga displayed, leading instructors from the Academy of Arts were brought to the Palace of Gatchina, where the Imperial family lived.

Olga had a special relationship with her father. They were soul mates. He was powerful, confident and authoritative, yet so happy, affectionate and comfortable in his family circle. He was everything to her and she adored him. It was a tragedy when he passed away in November 1894 at the age of 49 after seeming to have been ill for just a short period of time. It was only afterwards that the family remembered that he had already felt poorly and tired during the visit to Fredensborg, Denmark, in 1893. His condition had worsened during the winter but then his other daughter, the Grand Duchess Xenia, was to be married and that somehow pulled him through. The loss of her father was the first cruel blow fate would deal the twelve-year-old Olga. Many other hardships were to follow.

Alexander was succeeded by his eldest son Nicholas, who was in a state of panic about shouldering the heavy responsibility of ruling, which was passing to him.

Emperor Nicholas II
– mid-1890s.

He had not been taught statesmanship, but been trained as a soldier and had thus not been prepared for the throne. Nicholas was engaged to Princess Alix of Hesse, who rushed to his side to support him at the deathbed of his father. They married only a few days after the funeral. Five children were born: Olga in 1895, Tatiana in 1897, Maria in 1899, Anastasia in 1901 and Alexis in 1904.

When Olga was 19 her mother decided that it was time for her to be married. Usually Romanov girls left Russia to find an appropriate match abroad, but her mother wanted her to stay at home. A marriage was, therefore, arranged with Prince Peter of the Russian branch of the Oldenburg family, a long time family friend. Peter was 33, a gambler and reputedly homosexual.

Grand Duchess Olga Alexandrovna,
ca. 1900.

Olga and Peter were married on July 27th / August 9th, 1901, and moved into their own palace in St. Petersburg where they soon led separate lives. Peter continued his life of gambling surrounded by young men whilst Olga returned to her royal duties. They spent time each year with Peter's mother at her property Ramon, south of Moscow. The region so delighted Olga that she had her own property of Olgino built in the vicinity. In the spring of 1903 Olga went to a military review and her eyes fell on a tall fair man. He was Nicholas Kulikovsky, an officer. The two fell in love. It was May 9th, 1903 (in a letter to Nicholas dated May 8th, 1915, Olga writes: *"Tomorrow is our anniversary 9th May – the day when we told each other of our love with our eyes for the first time – do you remember? At the big luncheon?"*

Olga immediately told her husband that she did not love him and wanted a divorce so she could marry the man she loved. Peter said no, but made a concession. He hired Kulikovsky as an aide. Thus Olga and Nicholas could be near each other and wait for the possibility of a divorce, which could only be granted by her brother, the Emperor.

When the First World War broke out in 1914, Colonel Kulikovsky was commissioned to command the Akhtyrsky Hussars at Rovno, near the Polish-Austrian frontier. Olga immediately made preparations to leave the palace in St. Petersburg in order to nurse at the front-line. Throughout her time at the front in Rovno and later at Kiev, Olga continued to paint the scenes around her. She had a close relationship with both her mother, the Dowager Empress, and the Emperor and Empress and their children, whom she wrote to on a regular basis telling them about her work as a nurse.

Olga was also close to her sister Xenia and wrote a series of letters to her between the years 1916 and 1920 telling her about her life on the front and her hopes for a marriage to Nicholas Kulikovsky. In a letter dated August 30th / September 1st, 1916, Olga writes *"Xenia dear – I got a telegram last night from Nicky telling me I am free! It was a present from Papa – don't you think so? – just for his namesday – this rejoices me to believe it is he who helps"*. In the autumn of 1916, the Emperor came to inspect Olga's hospital in Kiev. There he gave her a handwritten letter in English annulling her marriage to Prince Peter and giving his blessing for her marriage to Colonel Kulikovsky. The marriage took place in the Vassilevskaya Church in Kiev on November 5th / 17th, 1916.

The year 1917 brought to an end over 300 years of Romanov rule in Russia. Revolution gripped the country, the Emperor was forced to abdicate and life became dangerous for the whole royal family. Olga and other members of the Imperial family fled to the Crimea to escape certain execution. There, at Ai-Todor, the estate of her brother-in-law Alexander Michailovich, Olga gave birth to her first son, Tihon. In late 1918 Olga was pregnant again and she and

The Cossack Timothy Ksenofontovich Yachik in uniform.

Hvidøre, where the Dowager Empress Marie Feodorovna and the Grand Duchess Olga Alexandrovna lived with her family till 1928.

Kulikovsky made a decision. Together with their son they left her mother in the Crimea to hide out in the Caucasus, an area not yet in Bolshevik hands. They were accompanied by Timothy Yachik, a Cossack servant, Mimka (Emilia Tenso),
Olga's maid, and Xenia Yakovlevna Moshaeva (a nurse from Olga's hospital). They settled in Yachik's home village of Novominskaya where Olga's second son Guri was born. It was here that Olga found her paradise. She no longer had her day organised for her, she felt at peace taking care of her family and growing her own vegetables. In a letter to Xenia dated March 26th, 1919, she writes: *We have made our kitchen garden & now I wait with impatience the signs of the appearance of the vegetables. I do love being near the earth! To feel near it all & live a life alone with it all.*

Father Leonid Kolchev.

After a period of relative calm, the Red offensive began against the Whites in the Caucasus, and the little family began their dangerous trek out of Russia. In Rostov-on-the Don, the Danish Consul gave them shelter and assisted with arrangements for them to leave the Caucasus for

Turkey. From there they travelled on to Serbia and Vienna and finally reached Copenhagen on Good Friday, April 2nd, 1920. There they first stayed with the Dowager Empress at Amalienborg Palace, and then moved to Hvidøre north of Copenhagen. This villa had been purchased by the Dowager Empress and her sister Queen Alexandra of England after the death of their father Christian IX in 1906, and became their official home in Denmark. It was here at Hvidøre that Tihon and Guri spent their childhood years. This period was neither easy for them nor for their parents. Olga was again living under her mother's thumb, running errands for her, receiving her guests and bearing her never-ending criticism. Xenia Yakovlevna Moshaeva became Tihon's and Guri's nanny. They called her

Watercolour by Grand Duchess Olga Alexandrovna of her sons, Tihon and Guri, 1920.

Avaka or Ava. The two boys did not go to a Danish school but had private tuition at home. Father Kolchev gave them religious instruction in Russian at the Alexander Nevski church in Copenhagen and was in due course replaced by his son Arkadi Kolchev. Every year Tihon and Guri were sent abroad for exams in Russian, first to Berlin and later to Paris.

A year after the family had arrived in Denmark Mimka turned up. She had made her way from St. Petersburg with Olga's jewels sewn into her clothes.

In the 1920s Olga asked the author Otto Schrayh to put the children's story of the three white bears into verse form and said that she would illustrate the story, which she did.

In October 1925 Olga went to Berlin with her husband to meet a woman who said she was Grand Duchess Anastasia Nicholaievna, the youngest daughter of her brother, the Emperor. This was the famous Anna Anderson who convinced many people that she was a member of the Romanov family. Olga did not recognise her though felt

From Grand Duchess Olga Alexandrovna's picture book "The Adventures of the Three White Bears".

*Grand Duchess Olga
Alexandrovna reading to her
godchild Olga Jacobsen.*

deeply sorry for the poor woman. Many years later, DNA tests confirmed Olga's opinion.

It was after the death of her sister – Queen Alexandra of England – that the Dowager Empress lost all zest for life. She passed away on October 13th, 1928, and was laid to rest in Roskilde. In 2006 she was reburied in the Peter and Paul Cathedral in St. Petersburg, next to her husband, Alexander III.

Olga inherited Hvidøre, but she had no intention of staying there. A public auction of the contents was held on April 9th, 1929, and the property was sold. Olga and her family leased the cottage of Rygaard in the old part of Holte while they looked for a suitable property. With her inheritance she purchased her own home "Knudsminde" in Ballerup, northwest of Copenhagen. There, Olga and Nicholas farmed and raised their two sons.

It was also at Knudsminde that Olga started a very happy and productive period of her artistic life. Her paintings through the mid-1940s reflect this with scene after scene of life on the 200-acre

Knudsminde.

farm. She made gifts of her artwork to members of her immediate Romanov family and also to her more extended Royal family. Today, paintings are to be found in the collections of Queen Elizabeth II of England, Queen Margrethe II of Denmark and King Harald V of Norway. In 1934 art dealer Richard Petersen arranged a most successful exhibition for Olga in his gallery in Copenhagen. In 1936, a selection of Olga's works of art was exhibited and sold at Agnews Gallery in London. The fifty paintings Olga had submitted were sold within two days. Over the years, exhibitions of her work were held in St. Petersburg, London, Copenhagen, Toronto, and at other places in Sweden, and Germany and more recently at the Smithsonian Institute and the Russian Ambassador's Residence in Washington, DC, the new Tretyakov Gallery in Moscow, and Kotka in Finland. A permanent exhibition can be viewed at the Ballerup Museum in Denmark.

Grand Duchess Olga Alexandrovna painting in the garden at Knudsminde in the 1940s.

After World War 2 broke out, Denmark was occupied by the Germans. Olga's life went on seemingly unchanged. Her two sons were growing up. She gave them the freedom to marry who they wanted to. They chose local girls. Guri married Ruth Schwartz in May 1940 and Tihon Agnete Pedersen in April 1942.

During the occupation the Germans brought Soviet prisoners of war to Denmark. With the collapse of Germany, Denmark was liberated by the British in May 1945. One part of Denmark, the island of Bornholm in the Baltic, was, however, liberated by the Red Army. The Soviets refused to leave and occupied the island for a year. They demanded the return of all Soviet citizens from Denmark. Anyone who was not sent back to the Soviet Union was considered a war criminal.

Olga found herself in a dangerous situation so she and Kulikovsky concluded that they would have to leave Denmark for the safety of faraway Canada.

It was May 10th, 1948, that found Olga, her husband, their two sons and daughters-in-law, her two grandchildren and faithful maid Mimka on their way to Esbjerg on the east coast of Jutland. From there they sailed to Harwich in England, where Queen Mary arranged for them to stay at Hampton Court. On June 2nd, they boarded "The Empress of Canada" at Liverpool for the voyage to

May 1948: the Kulikovsky family just before their departure for Canada.

Canada where they landed after a rough crossing on June 9th. They settled on a farm by the name of Nassaguja in Campbellville in the vast, flat countryside outside Toronto. The scene inspired Olga and reminded her of Imperial Russia, as well as of Denmark. She continued painting, sending much of her artwork back to Copenhagen to be sold. In 1952 the upkeep of the farm had become a burden and the farm was sold. Olga and Nicholas retired to a smaller home in Cooksville, closer to Toronto. There, in 1958, Nicholas died. He was buried in the Russian section of York Cemetery in Toronto. Olga, declining in health, remained in the Cooksville home surrounded by her artwork and the many Romanov family treasures she had so carefully looked after through revolution and exile.

Emilie Tenso's (Mimka) Alien's Passport, stamped for Canadian Immigration.

In April of 1960, Olga fell seriously ill and was hospitalized in Toronto. When discharged, she was taken in and cared for by close friends in their flat above their barbershop in Toronto. She died there on November 24th, 1960, at the age of 78. Her remains were moved to the Russian Cathedral of Christ the Saviour in Toronto, where she lay in state for five days, four giant incense candles burning continuously. The open

Indehaverens Underskrift
Signature du porteur
Signature of the bearer
Unterschrift des Passinhabers

Grand Duchess Olga Alexandrovna's Danish Passport, stamped for Canadian Immigration.

coffin with the Imperial standard draping it stood on a catafalque surrounded by sheer walls of flowers. Standing guard at each end of the coffin were members of both Nicholas' Cuirassier Regiment and Olga's Akhtyrsky Regiment. An exquisite piece of silver and gold embroidery with the Imperial crown and the cipher O.A. for Olga Alexandrovna lay at the foot of the coffin. On November 30th, 1960, more than five hundred mourners filled the Cathedral. The Requiem Mass was followed by a short memorial sermon by Bishop Athenagoras, head of the Greek Church in Canada. Representatives of Orthodox communities took part in the service. After the last homage had been paid, the coffin was closed. It was covered with the Imperial standard and the old regimental colours that had been brought over to Canada by a Hussar not long after the Revolution. Many royal names appeared on the wreaths. Olga's kin from all over Europe had remembered her, and a Romanov cousin of hers, Princess Vera of Russia, came over from New York. After a three-hour service, the procession drove to York Cemetery under a slate grey sky to lay Olga's body beside her beloved Nicholas, and yards away from her faithful servant Mimka.

Olga had not been forgotten in Denmark. A prayer for her salvation was said at the Alexander Nevski Church in Copenhagen on November 27th.

Grand Duchess Olga and Colonel N. A Kulikovsky's grave in North York Cemetery, Toronto, Canada.

Karen Roth-Nicholls and Sue Woolmans

197

List of Letters and Book Excerpts

Bibliography

Grand Duchess Olga Alexandrovna – Complete Handwritten Notes.

Grand Duchess Olga Alexandrovna – "*Storfyrstinde Olga – 25 kapitler af mit liv*" (*Grand Duchess Olga – 25 Chapters of my Life*), Aschehoug Dansk Forlag, Copenhagen, 2006 and 2007.

Bruun-Rasmussen, Copenhagen – *Auction Catalogue*, December 2007.

Maria Feodorovna – *Catalogue Exhibition Christiansborg Palace*, Copenhagen 1997.

Mengden, Zinaide – "*Grevinde Zinaide Mengdens Erindringer*" (*The Memoirs of Countess Zinaide Mengden*), Ida Wennerberg, H. Hagerup, Copenhagen, 1943.

Neerbek, Hans – "*Tihon, the Tsar's Nephew*", Rosvall Royal Books, Sweden, 2005.

Phenix, Patricia – "*Olga Romanov – Russia's Last Grand Duchess*", Viking, Penguin Books Canada Limited, Toronto, 1999.

Pridham, Francis – "*Close of a Dynasty*", Allan Wingate (Publishers) Limited, London, 1956

Romanoff, Roman –"*Det var et rigt hus, et lykkeligt hus – Erindringer af Roman Romanoff, prins af Rusland, 1896–1919*" (*The Memoirs of Roman Romanoff, Prince of Russia*), Gyldendal, Copenhagen, 1991.

Ulstrup, Preben – "*Kejserinde Dagmars fangenskab paa Krim, dagbøger og breve*" ("*The Captivity of the Empress Dagmar in the Crimea, Diaries and Letters*), Gyldendal, Copenhagen, 2005.

Vorres, Ian – "*The Last Grand Duchess – Her Imperial Highness Grand-Duchess Olga Alexandrovna*", Hutchinson of London, 2001.

Зверева Н. К. – "Августейшие Сестры Милосердия", Москва "Вече", 2006 (Zvereva H.K. "*August Sisters of Mercy*", Moscow, Verche, 2006).

Земляниченко Марина / Николай Калинин – "Романовы и Крым", Симферополь Бизнес Информ, 2007 (Marina Zemljanitschenko, Nikolaj Kalinin – "*The Romanovs in the Crimea*", Simferopol Business Inform, 2007)

Recommended Reading

Alexander, Grand Duke – "*Once a Grand Duke*", Cassell, London, 1932.

Alexander, Grand Duke – "*Always a Grand Duke*", Cassell, London, 1933.

Aronson, Theo – "*A Family of Kings – The Descendants of Christian IX of Denmark*", Cassell, London, 1976.

Belyakova, Zoia – "*A Strange Prince – Prince Peter of Oldenburg and Grand Duchess Olga Alexandrovna*", Royalty Digest Quarterly 2007.

Bramsen, Bo. – "*Huset Glücksborg – Europas svigerfader og hans efterslægt*" (*The House of Glucksburg – the Father-in-Law of Europe and his Descendants*), Forum, Copenhagen, 1992.

Crawford, Rosemary & Donald – "*Michael and Natasha*", Weidenfeld & Nicolson, London 1977.

Hall, Coryne – "*Little Mother of Russia – A Biography of Empress Marie Feodorovna*", Shepheard-Walwyn, London 1999.

Klausen, Inger-Lise – "*Dagmar, Zarina fra Danmark*" (*Dagmar, the Danish Tsarina*), Lindhardt & Ringhof, Copenhagen, 1997.

Lerche, Anna and Mandal, Marcus – "*A Royal Family. The Story of Christian IX and his European Descendants*", Preface by her Majesty Queen Margrethe II, Aschehoug, Copenhagen, 2003.

Madol, Hans Roger – "*Christian IX*", Collins, London, 1939.

Tisdall, E.E.P – "*Marie Feodorovna, Empress of Russia*", Stanley Paul, London, 1957.

Van der Kiste, John and Hall, Coryne – "*Once a Grand Duchess – Xenia, Sister of Nicholas II*", Sutton Publishing Ltd, Stroud, Gloucestershire, 2002.

Van der Kiste, John – "*The Romanovs 1818–1959*", Sutton Publishing Ltd, Stroud, Gloucestershire, 1998.

Yaschik, Timothy Ksenofontovich – "*En livkosaks Erindringer*" (*The Memoirs of a Life Cossack*), Zac, Copenhagen 1968. Russian editions in 2004 and 2007 published by Nestor-Historia, Saint Petersburg.

Zeepvat, Charlotte – "*The Camera and the Tsars*", Sutton Publishing Ltd, Stroud, Gloucestershire, 2004.

Zeepvat, Charlotte – "*Romanov Autumn*", Sutton Publishing Ltd, Stroud, Gloucestershire, 2000.

Index of People and Places

AAGE

Prince of Denmark, son of Prince Valdemar and Princess Marie, born 1887, married 1914 to Mathilde Calvi di Bergolo, died 1940. GD Olga's cousin. Page 48.

ABBAS-TOUMAN

A mountain village in the Caucasus where GD George Alexandrovich lived from 1891 till his death in 1899. Pages 51–52, 54.

AKHTYRSKY REGIMENT

In 1901 GD Olga was appointed honorary Commander-in-Chief of the Twelfth Akhtyrsky Hussar Regiment. Pages 117–118, 120, 124, 127, 197.

AI-PETRI

The highest point of the mountain range behind the Ai-Todor estate in the Crimea. Page 150.

AI-TODOR

The summer residence in the Crimea of GD Alexander Michaelovich (Anitchkov). Pages 143–145, 147, 149–153, 159, 160–162, 191.

ALEXANDER OF OLDENBURG

Prince of Russia, born 1844, married 1868 to Eugenie Maximilianovna, Princess of Leuchtenberg, died 1932. GD Olga's first father-in-law. Pages 67–70, 190.

ALEXANDER MICHAELOVICH (SANDRO)

Grand Duke of Russia, born 1866, married 1894 to GD Xenia Alexandrovna, died 1933. GD Olga's brother-in-law. Pages 45–47, 57, 59, 92, 109, 112, 129, 134, 136, 138–139, 143, 147, 149, 160–161, 191.

ALEXANDER I

1888–1934, King of Yugoslavia 1921–1934, previously King of the Serbs, Croats and Slovenes, 1922 married to HRH Princess Maria of Romania. Assassinated. Page 175.

ALEXANDER III

Emperor of Russia, born 1845 in St. Petersburg, married 1866 to Princess Dagmar of Denmark, succeeded his father Alexander II after his assassination 1881 and crowned in Moscow 1883. Died 1894 in Livadia. GD Olga's father. Pages 12–13, 15–16, 20–21, 24–27, 30–33, 37, 43–48, 52, 117, 189–190, 194.

ALEXANDRA (ALIX)
: Queen of England, born 1844 as Princess of Denmark, married 1863 to Edward, Prince of Wales (later King Edward VII), died 1925, sister to the Empress Marie Feodorovna (Dagmar) and GD Olga's maternal aunt. Pages 16–17, 19, 83, 102, 156, 193–194.

ALEXANDRA FEODOROVNA (ALICKY)
: Empress, born 1872 as Alexandra of Hesse, married 1894 to Nicholas II, took the Russian name Alexandra Feodorovna, assassinated 1918. GD Olga's sister-in-law. Pages 19, 47, 65, 73–74, 79, 81, 99, 110.

ALEXANDRA NICHOLAIEVNA
: Grand Duchess of Russia and daughter of the Emperor Nicholas I, born 1825, married 1844 to Friedrich, Prince of Hesse, died 1844. Brother of Queen Louise of Denmark. Pages 97.

ALEXANDRINE
: Queen of Denmark, born 1879, married 1898 to Crown Prince Christian of Denmark (later King Christian X), died 1952. Page 56.

ALEXIS NICHOLAIEVICH (ALEXEI)
: Tsarevich of Russia, son of Emperor Nicholas II and Empress Alexandra Feodorovna, born 1904, assassinated 1918. GD Olga's nephew. Pages 73, 76, 97, 99, 101, 114, 131, 190.

AMDRUP, GEORGE CARL
: Danish Vice Admiral and Greenland explorer, born 1866, died 1947. Page 13.

ANASTASIA MICHAELOVNA
: Grand Duchess of Russia, daughter of GD Michael Nicholaievich, born 1860, married 1879 to Friedrich Franz of Mecklenburg-Schwerin, died 1922. Mother of Queen Alexandrine of Denmark. Page 56.

ANITCHKOV PALACE
: The residence of the Empress Marie Feodorovna on the Nevski Prospect in St. Petersburg. Pages 20, 30.

AXEL
: Prince of Denmark, son of Prince Valdemar and Princess Marie, born 1888, married 1919 to Margaretha, Princess of Sweden, died 1964. GD Olga's cousin. Page 48.

CHARLOTTENLUND PALACE
  The summer residence of Crown Prince Frederick of Denmark (later King Frederik VIII), north of Copenhagen. Page 49.

CHRISTIAN IX
  King of Denmark, born 1818, married 1842 to Princess Louise of Hesse-Cassel, died 1906. GD Olga's grandfather. Pages 17–19, 48–49, 193.

CHRISTIAN
  Prince of Denmark, later King Christian X. Pages 18–19, 45.

CHRISTIAN X
  King of Denmark from 1912, born 1870, married 1898 to Alexandrine, Princess of Mecklenburg-Schwerin, died 1947. GD Olga's cousin. Page 18.

CHRISTIANIA FJORD
  Now Oslo Fjord. Page 83.

CONSTANTINOPLE
  Conquered by the Ottomans in 1453 and the capital of their empire until 1922. The city was officially renamed Istanbul by the Turkish Republic in 1930. Pages 156, 174–175.

COSSACKS
  A people living in the southern steppe regions of Russia, famous for their self-reliance and military skills, particularly horsemanship. Pages 31, 33, 54, 76, 80, 115, 147, 134, 164, 167, 173, 192, .

CRIMEA
  A peninsula in the Ukraine on the northern coast of the Black Sea. Pages 16, 21, 26, 32, 48, 143, 147, 150, 155–157, 161–163, 176, 191–192.

CUIRASSIER REGIMENT
  A cavalry regiment established in 1704 by Peter the Great. Empress Marie Feodorovna was its honorary Commander-in-Chief. GD Olga's second husband, Nicholas Kulikovsky, was an officer in the regiment. Pages 89, 91–92, 136, 197.

DANUBE RIVER
  A 2,850 km long river and Europe's second-longest river after the Volga. It originates in the Black Forest in Germany and flows generally eastwards, emptying into the Black Sea in Romania. Page 175.

ESCAILLE, SIDONIE
de l'Escaille, Sidonie 1932–1922. Belgian governess and Lady-in-Waiting to the Empress Marie Feodorovna. Pages 33–34.

EUGENIE MAXIMILIANOVNA
Princess Romanovsky, Duchess of Leuchtenberg born 1845, married to Alexander Duke of Oldenburg, died 1925. GD Olga's first mother-in-law. Pages 109–110.

THE FARM
A large three-storey stone palace located near the Cottage in the Alexandria Park in Peterhof and used by Emperor Alexander II as a private residence. Page 81.

FRANCKLIN, ELIZABETH (NANA)
GD Olga's English nanny, born 1834, married 1858 to Thomas Francklin, England, died 1913 in St. Petersburg. Pages 13, 22, 25, 32, 37, 39, 43, 72, 85–86.

FREDENSBORG CASTLE
A palace north-west of Copenhagen and often used for family reunions by King Christian IX. Pages 17, 19, 21, 46, 189.

FREDERICKS, VLADIMIR
Russian baron, Court Marshal and Minister of the Imperial Court, 1838–1927. Page 75.

FREDERICK VIII
1843–1912. Crown Prince, King of Denmark 1906, married 1869 to Princess Lovisa of Sweden, GD Olga's cousin. Pages 17, 19.

GAGRY
A town in the Abkhazian region of western Georgia on the north-east coast of the Black Sea at the foot of the Caucasus Mountains. Pages 68–71.

GATCHINA
A town and palace 45 km south of St. Petersburg. Pages 13, 15, 20, 27, 30, 32–33, 40–41, 43, 54, 56–57, 89, 92, 95–96, 112, 117, 189.

KAMENETZ-PODOLSK
A town in the Ukraine, south of Rovno and south-west of Kiev. Page 125.

KAMTCHATCA
Emperor Alexander III's favourite dog, which lost its life in the Borki disaster in 1888. Page 24.

KARLSBAD (KARLOVZ VARY)
A town west of Prague and known as an internationally famous spa for its medicinal hot spring waters. Page 85.

KHARKOV
A town in north-east Ukraine. Pages 22, 25, 115, 135.

KIEV
The capital of the Ukraine. The government has its seat in the Maryinsky Palace, which was the property of the Imperial family till 1917. Pages 95, 104, 110, 119, 128, 130–136, 138, 140, 142–143, 147, 150, 176, 191.

KNUDSMINDE
A large farm in Ballerup, Denmark, where Grand Duchess Olga lived with her family from 1930–1948. Demolished. Pages 11–12, 36, 194–195.

KREBS, DR. CARL IMMANUEL
Danish doctor 1889–1971. Transferred to Russia by the Danish Red Cross and sent by Harald Scavenius, the Danish Ambassador in St. Petersburg, to the Dowager Empress Marie Feodorovna in the Crimea, bringing her money and food. Pages 155, 161.

KRONSTADT
An island in the Gulf of Finland, 30 km west of St. Petersburg, served as the base of the Russian Baltic Fleet and was the seat of the Russian admiralty. Page 13.

KUBAN
A rich farming region in the northern Caucasus. Cossacks were settled in the region around the Kuban River to protect the southern borders of the Russian Empire. Pages 115, 164, 167.

KULIKOVSKY, GURI
Grand Duchess Olga's younger son, born 1919, named after Guri Panaev, married 1940 to Ruth Schwartz, died 1984. Pages 157, 164–165, 176, 178, 192–193, 195.

MARIE FEODOROVNA (DAGMAR)
Danish Princess, daughter of King Christian IX and Queen Louise of Denmark, born 1847, married 1866 to Grand Duke Alexander Alexandrovich of Russia (later Emperor Alexander III), took the Russian name Marie Feodorovna, died 1928, Grand Duchess Olga Alexandrovna's mother. Pages 15–17, 19–21, 24–26, 29–35, 37, 43–46, 48–49, 51, 53–54, 82, 89–90, 92–93, 102, 108, 111, 130, 134, 138–139, 142–146, 150–152, 155–156, 163, 176–177, 189–190, 192–194.

MARIE (MISSY)
Queen of Romania, born 1875, Princess of Sachsen-Coburg and Gotha, married 1893 to Ferdinand, Crown Prince of Romania, from 1914 King of Romania, died 1938. Page 155.

MAUD
English Princess, born 1869, daughter of Edward VII and Queen Alexandra, married 1896 to Prince Carl of Denmark (later King Haakon VII of Norway), died 1938. GD Olga's cousin. Pages 19, 45.

MEDZIBOSH
A medieval fortress in South Poland and the headquarters of the Akhtyrsky Regiment. Pages 117–118.

MICHAEL ALEXANDROVICH (MISHA)
Grand Duke of Russia, born 1878, Tsarevich 1899–1904, married 1912 to Natalie Sergeyevna Sheremetevskaya, assassinated 1918. GD Olga's elder brother. Pages 12, 14, 16, 19–20, 27–28, 30, 33, 37, 39–41, 43–44, 48, 51–53, 85–86, 89–95.

MICHAEL NICHOLAIEVICH
Grand Duke of Russia, born 1832, married 1857 to Cecilie, Princess of Baden, died 1909. GD Xenia's father-in-law. Page 56.

MOGHILEV
Military headquarters, where Emperor Nicholas II and Empress Marie Feodorovna met for the last time. Now in Belarus. Pages 143, 147.

MORDVINOV, A.
ADC in the Imperial Cuirassier Regiment. Pages 92, 114.

NANA
See Francklin.

OREL
A village 650 km south of Moscow, where Grand Duke Michael
Alexandrovich was stationed as Colonel of a cavalry regiment. Pages 89, 93.

OZEROVA, CATHERINE
Maid and Lady-in-Waiting to the Empress Marie Feodorovna. Page 34.

PANAEV BORIS, GURI AND LEV
Officers in the Akhtyrsky Regiment. Grand Duchess Olga's youngest son
was named after Guri, who was killed in combat 29.08.1914 and buried
in the village of Demnia outside Lvov. Pages 119, 122, 157.

PASTEUR, LOUIS
French micro-biologist. 1822–1895. Page 67.

PAUL I
Emperor of Russia, born 1754, married 1773 to Princess Wilhelmina of
Hesse-Darmstadt, who took the Russian name Natalia Alexeievna, and
then in 1776 to Duchess Sophie-Dorothea of Würtemberg, who took the
Russian name Maria Feodorovna, assassinated 1801. Page 96.

PENZING HAUS
The residence of Duchess Thyra of Cumberland in the 14th district
of Vienna. Page 176.

PERA
The main street in Constantinople. Page 175.

PERUN
Heathen god of lightning and thunder. Page 134.

PETER NICHOLAIEVICH
Grand Duke of Russia, born 1864, married 1889 to Militza, Princess
of Montenegro, died 1931. Pages 151, 153.

PETER OF OLDENBURG
Prince of Russia, born 1868, married 1901 to Grand Duchess Olga,
divorced 1916, died 1924. Pages 19, 56–58, 83, 190–191.

PETER THE GREAT
Emperor of Russia, born 1672, married 1689 to Eudokia Feodorovna
Lopouhine and 1711 to Martha Skavronska, who took the Russian name
Ekatarina Alexeievna, died 1725. Page 60.

SAROV
A town 250 km south-east of Moscow. Pages 64–65.

SANDRO
See Alexander Michaelovich.

SCHACK-SOMMER
An English volunteer in the Akhtyrsky Regiment. Page 127.

SCHYTTE, THOMAS
The Danish consul in Novorossisk. Pages 173, 176.

SERAPHIM
A Russian saint and priest in Sarov. 1759–1833. Pages 64–66.

SEVASTOPOL
A port on the Black Sea coast of the Crimea. Pages 51, 113, 144–145, 149,
152–153, 160.

SHEREMETEV, VLADIMIR ALEXEIEVICH
Russian Colonel, born 1847, married 1879 to Helena Grigorrevna
Countess Stroganova, died 1893. Page 24.

SNJIATIN
A village near Proskurov in the Bukovina in south-east Ukraine.
Pages 126–127.

THE SOPHIA MOSQUE
Called Hagia Sophia (Church of Holy Wisdom). Built in the 6th century
by the Emperor Justinian as a Christian church and converted into a
mosque in 1463 when the Turks conquered Constantinople. Converted
into a museum in 1935. Page 175.

SORRENTO
A town south of Naples in Italy. Pages 85–86.

THE STANDART
An Imperial yacht, built by Burmeister & Wain in Copenhagen, ordered
1893 and delivered 1895. Pages 97–99.

TATIANA NICHOLAIEVNA
Grand Duchess of Russia and daughter of Emperor Nicholas II and
Alexandra Feodorovna , born 1897, assassinated 1918. Pages 19, 73, 75,
109–110, 112, 122, 128, 136–137, 190.

VICTORIA
English Princess born 1868, daughter of King Edward VII and Queen Alexandra, unmarried, died 1935. GD Olga's cousin. Pages 16, 19, 45, 83.

VIGGO
Danish Prince, born 1893, son of Prince Valdemar and Princess Marie, from 1923 Count of Rosenborg, married 1924 to Eleanor Green, died 1970. GD Olga's cousin. Pages 18, 48–49.

VLADIMIR, St
Grand Prince of Kiev, ca. 956 – 1015, introduced Christianity in Russia in AD 988 in its Eastern, or Greek, form rather than its Western, or Roman, form. Page 104.

XENIA ALEXANDROVNA
Grand Duchess of Russia, born 1875, married 1894 to GD Alexander Michaelovich (Sandro), died 1960. GD Olga's elder sister. Pages 12, 16, 20, 44–47, 56, 59, 92, 108–109, 111, 143–144, 151, 161–163, 189, 191–192.

YACHIK, TIMOTHY
1878–1946. Empress Dagmar's Cossack bodyguard, who accompanied her to Denmark and settled there after her death. Pages 134, 139, 147, 191–192.

YALTA
A town on the southern coast of the Crimean peninsula in the Ukraine. Pages 145, 152, 159–160, 162–163.

YANISHEV, IOANN
1826–1910. Professor of theology at St. Petersburg University. He came to Fredensborg in 1864 to give Dagmar lessons in the Russian language and prepare her for conversion to the Orthodox faith. He had served as a priest in Orthodox churches in Berlin and Wiesbaden and later became Confessor to the Imperial Family. He was awarded the Order of Merit of Duke Peter Friedrich Ludwig of Oldenburg in 1901 at the time of Olga's marriage to Prince Peter of Oldenburg. Pages 21, 72.